Adolescence
Is Not an Illness

Adolescence Is Not an Illness

Bruce Narramore, Ph.D.

ILLUSTRATIONS *by Diane Head*

Fleming H. Revell Company
Old Tappan, New Jersey

Library of Congress Cataloging in Publication Data

Narramore, Bruce.
    Adolescence is not an illness.

    Includes index.
    1. Adolescence.   2. Adolescent psychology.
3. Parenting. I. Title.
HQ793.N37   305.2'3   80-10170
ISBN 0-8007-5101-9

Contents

Part I Understanding Your Teen

1 A New Beginning   9
2 "What's Happening to My Body?"   15
3 Awakening Sexuality   21
4 Fluctuating Moods   27
5 Peer Pressure   31
6 The Drive for Independence   35
7 "I've Got to Find Myself"   39

Part II Guidelines for Growth

8 Accept your Teenager's Anxiety and
   Discontent   47
9 Never Argue With a Feeling   55
10 Be Sensitive to Sensitive Areas   59
11 Be Reasonable, Dad! (And Mom)   63
12 Yes, No, and Maybe So   71
13 Let's Be Friends   75
14 Fragile Egos: Handle With Respect   80

Part III Common Conflicts

15 Coping With Peer Pressure   89
16 Dating   96

17	Sex in Adolescence	105
18	Disciplining Adolescents	112
19	Alcohol and Drugs	121
20	Disinterest in Church	128
21	Money Matters	136
22	Coping With Conflict	141
23	Teenage Negativism	147
24	Post-High-School Years	154
25	What to Do After You've Blown It!	160
Index		172

Part I

Understanding Your Teen

1

A New Beginning

During a lively parental discussion of some of the problems encountered in the teenage years, a frustrated mother exclaimed, "I guess I look at adolescence the same way I did the childhood illnesses, like measles, mumps, and chicken pox. I knew our children would eventually catch them and I just prayed they would have a 'light case' and recover quickly! But now I'm getting worried. We hear these horror stories from other parents and really wonder what we're in for."

Like this mother, most parents of adolescents feel at least a tinge of anxiety over their teenager's adjustment in the next few years. We hear stories of blatant disrespect for authority, of widespread alcohol and drug use, loud music, and unintelligible communication. We recall the warning: "Just wait until your kids are teenagers!" And now we realize the time is here! Coupled with memories of our own adolescent struggles, or those of our acquaintances, these somber warnings do little to build a positive attitude toward parenting an adolescent. We may fear that happy family times are gone forever—or at least until our children pass through this dreadful stage and regain their sanity!

Fortunately, these dire predictions need not come true. Adolescence is neither an illness nor a confirmed disaster area. Some parents and teenagers have fabulous times together. Many never encounter really serious conflicts or major crises. And others weather the predictable storms of adolescence without too much disharmony or pain. In fact, adolescence can bring some of the most rewarding moments parents ever experience.

Joyce, the mother of two teenage daughters, expressed it this way: "I love every minute of it. I love sharing with them, crying with them, going places with them, and look forward to the special times we have together. People sometimes say, 'Aren't teenagers difficult?' and I think, *Difficult? In what way?* Each new phase in our teenagers' lives has been surprising, special, and rewarding, so I hardly noticed the difficulties."

Our teenager's first date, first car, and first paycheck can be especially satisfying times. And the teenager's first romantic breakup, the first big disappointment, or the first major emergency can bring the family together in ways that usually do not happen when things are running smoothly.

Later adolescent years provide opportunities for seeing our offspring reach out on their own, test their wings, and advance toward responsible adulthood. This is a rewarding time for parents who are prepared to enjoy the process—to see our previously dependent children move to the point at which they are ready to step out on their own. Christian parents have the added prospect of seeing our teenagers' faith mature into a powerful, integrating force in their lives.

The teen years do, of course, present some special challenges and unique problems for both teenagers and their parents. The path from dependent childhood to proficient adulthood is beset with real-life obstacles. And the differing perceptions of parents and teens guarantee a certain amount of friction and tension. But these conflicts needn't rupture relationships. A little patience and understanding can restore calm and forge unity for another period of peace. We don't have to throw up our hands in despair.

When problems arise, there are some specific steps we can

take for resolution. In fact, the adolescent years give us an excellent opportunity—perhaps our last—to repair any psychological damage done in the first decade or so of life. Now that our children are older, we can seek new solutions to old problems, mend some old wounds, and remove old barriers to communication and understanding. To achieve this, however, we need to exercise or develop five basic attitudes or parenting skills. These are:

1. the ability to understand our teenagers' world of thoughts, feelings, conflicts, and experience;
2. the ability to communicate respect and love to our teenagers in ways they can understand and receive;
3. the ability to enjoy our teenagers and spend mutually rewarding times together;
4. the ability to resolve problems, conflicts, and misunderstandings;
5. the ability to accept ourselves and to realize there are no "perfect parents."

Several years ago our family was visiting the Grand Canyon. In the curio shop I noticed a small plaque bearing an "Indian Prayer." It read:

GREAT SPIRIT, HELP ME NOT TO CRITICIZE MY BROTHER TILL
I HAVE WALKED A MILE IN HIS MOCCASINS.

That is a pertinent plea for parents of teenagers. Perhaps the single most important quality for effective parenting is the ability to see things from our teenagers' perspectives. Only as we understand our sons' and daughters' ways of looking at things and the attitudes and feelings they are experiencing, will we be able to help them through the sometimes tumultuous years of adolescence.

In the first seven chapters of this book, I want to step into our teenagers' shoes and recall what it is like to be a teen. We will look at some of the struggles every teenager faces and probe some of the developments that often generate conflicts in the second decade of life. We will do this by examining several common characteristics of adolescence and some of the important developmental tasks teenagers face.

Based on our understanding of these struggles, Part II will suggest seven guidelines for building and maintaining good relations with adolescent sons and daughters. These guidelines are essentially suggestions for communicating a deep sense of respect for our teenagers and for learning to enjoy each other's company. They won't magically resolve all the problems we will encounter, but, if put into practice, they can go a long way toward insuring a relatively smooth trip through adolescence!

No matter how well we come to understand our teenagers, however, and no matter how deeply we learn to enjoy and respect them, we cannot eliminate all conflicts, problems, and frustrations. Effective parenting requires the facing of these problems and working toward mutually satisfying solutions. In Part III, we will consider ten of the most perplexing situations faced by parents of adolescents—problems concerning dating, sex, negativism, drugs, and similar issues. In each we will look at some probable causes of the problem and some guidelines for coping with it.

In conclusion, we will discuss one of the most difficult questions I have ever been asked. That question is: "What do we do after we've blown it?" After our sons and daughters are grown— or nearly so—and we can see the effects of some long-term problems in our family living, *is there anything we can do?* Must we continue to berate and condemn ourselves for our failures? Do we just sit back and pray? Or what?

Living with teenagers isn't always easy. But for that matter neither is living with a parent! My goal is to help parents maximize the good times we have with our growing adolescents, to avoid or solve some potentially serious problems, and to learn to live gracefully with some inevitable misunderstandings, conflicts, and disagreements. In the words of a well-known prayer:

> God, grant me the serenity to accept what I cannot
> change,
> Courage to change the things I can,
> And the wisdom to know the difference.

One of the things we often cannot change immediately is ourselves. As you read these pages, I would like to suggest that you approach the concepts and suggestions as *guidelines* for growth and understanding, rather than as one more set of standards by which to judge your adequacy as a parent! None of us is a perfect parent, and many of us tend to be very hard on ourselves. We focus more on our failures and mistakes than we do on our successes and strengths.

If you are a bit that way, you may have a tendency to feel even more guilty after hearing another lecture or reading another book on parenting. But that is a self-defeating cycle. We need to face the fact that all of us make mistakes, and that there will always be some things we wish we had handled differently. Yet, in spite of this, we can accept ourselves and approach our parenting with positive attitudes. When we lose our tempers or do or say something we regret later, we can acknowledge it, apologize to our offspring—and move ahead. We can also set directions for growth that will allow us to overcome that type of negative reaction in the future. Our teenagers do not expect us to be perfect— but they do want us to be honest about our own needs—and willing to accept our part of the responsibility for family growth and harmony.

As I penned these pages, I have also kept in mind the parents of preteen youngsters, since it won't be long until their offspring reach the magical age of adolescence—and a little advance preparation can never hurt!

With this brief introduction, let's move right into our discussion of what makes teenagers tick and try to see why they are sometimes so difficult to understand.

2

"What's Happening to My Body?"

Do you remember how you felt about your body when you were a thirteen- or fourteen-year-old? Can you honestly say you liked everything about it? Was your complexion clear? Was your height okay, and your weight apportioned impressively? Did your ears and eyes and nose inspire at least your admiration? In short, did you like everything about yourself?

Most of us didn't. We felt too tall or too short, too heavy or too skinny, too clumsy or too pimply—or too something else. And the way we felt about our bodies affected many areas of our lives.

The rapid physical changes in teenagers and preteens are so natural that we can overlook their emotional importance. Yet these changes are the basis of most of the personality changes our adolescents go through and many problems they encounter. A year or so before puberty (physiological sexual maturity), most adolescents begin a period of rapid physical growth. They shoot up in height. Baby fat begins to disappear. Girls' breasts begin to develop. Pubic hair appears. Boys' testes enlarge and their voices begin to deepen.

While there is no set age for these changes, they generally begin at about nine or ten for girls and a couple of years later for boys. Since girls usually experience this prepubertal-growth spurt earlier than their male counterparts, they may temporarily surpass their male peers in size. This advantage lasts for a couple of years, until the average boy generally catches up and passes the girls his age.

Because twelve- and thirteen-year-old girls are often more mature than boys their own age, they are usually not too interested in males in their own grade levels. They are more likely to be enamored of the older boys—one, two, or even three years ahead in school. Just recently I overheard two teenage girls discussing their boyfriends in a conversation that went:

13-YEAR-OLD   He's seventeen.
15-YEAR-OLD   That's great. That's just the right age.
13-YEAR-OLD   Yeah. The guys thirteen are so short.
15-YEAR-OLD   Yeah. The guys my age have started to grow but they are *so* immature.

This typical conversation demonstrates the social importance of physical size and maturity. Our teenagers' social relationships, as well as their feelings about themselves, are closely linked to their physical maturity.

At about twelve years for girls and fourteen for boys, these physical changes culminate in physical sexual maturity. Most girls by this age have been having menstrual periods for some time and are sexually fertile. The boys are also fertile and capable of ejaculating semen. These changes produce myriad new feelings in early teens. Although they have been eagerly anticipated (by most), they are also vaguely feared and deviations from "the average" can be especially upsetting—unless, of course, they vary in the accepted direction!

Research indicates that early-maturing boys are generally better adjusted personally and socially than "late bloomers." Their

physical advantages tend to promote athletic success, greater appeal to the opposite sex, and greater social desirability.

Any physical development that puts a teenager conspicuously out of sync with himself or his friends, however, can become a serious problem. Take Carl, for example. A tall, gangling fifteen-year-old, Carl shot up three or four inches in height in a short time. When he tried out for basketball, the coach was thrilled. Carl has the height to be a strong forward. Unfortunately, he had grown so quickly, his coordination has lagged behind his size. He is tall, gangly and awkward and has trouble getting both feet going in the same direction at the same time! Though he skipped rope, jogged through inner tubes, and tried all sorts of calisthenics, nothing cured his handicap. Soon his friends began to tease him about his height and his awkwardness. They asked if they could borrow his shoes for skis or help him down the stairs. Although these comments seemed humorous, and Carl tried to laugh them off, they hurt inside. He began to feel even more awkward and his self-image came under attack. Carl knows he is different from the other kids. He is growing so fast his parents can't keep him in clothes, and he even looks a little funny. At this point in his life he needs a lot of encouragement and support, not ridicule or teasing.

Since feelings of awkwardness and being different are painful, many teenagers like Carl will try to compensate. They turn into a cutup or a clown to shift attention from their peculiarity. They become a "tough guy" to shield their inner sensitivity; or they withdraw physically or emotionally to isolate their hurt.

The heavyweight boy has his own built-in problem. The football coach sees him and hopes he has a tackle or a guard for his defensive line. But the "incredible hulk" is just too slow—like molasses on a winter morning. He can plug a hole in the line—if he can get there in time. But arriving before the ball carrier is quite a problem. Before long his coach or teammates are "on his case." They yell, "Move it, Fatso. Get the lead out!" Or, "Come on, Lard; fire it up!" Whatever the epithet, it demeans his self-esteem. He shrinks inwardly, yearning to be like the other guys.

The undersized boy faces similar conflicts. He is labeled "Shrimp," "Shorty" or "Runt." He feels small enough without the reminders, and these labels make him feel like the proverbial ninety-pound weakling. He gulps extra helpings of potatoes and other starches to put on weight. He lifts weights and strains at his calisthenics. But the so-called average boy still overshadows him. This makes him doubt his masculinity and undermines his confidence. It can make him hesitant socially and stir a conglomeration of negative emotions.

Girls endure similar dilemmas. Unusual height, flat chests, and large frames may be severe burdens. Just recently the mother of a fourteen-year-old told me, "Our daughter is likable, attractive, and bright, but some kids tease her unmercifully, because she is still flat-chested. She comes home in tears and retreats to her room." Yes, it hurts teens to be different from their friends.

Because of the wide-ranging impact physical development has on teenagers' attitudes towards themselves, mirrors serve overtime duty during their changing years. Girls check out their overall attractiveness, their breast development, and the progress of their curves. A boy looks in the same mirror to flex his biceps, inspect his beard, or check out the size and shape of his penis and testes. If the mirrors record at least an "average" score, the viewers judge themselves as adequate, compared to their peers. If they sense inferiorities in size or line, they doubt their masculinity (or femininity) and fear the judgments of their peers.

Acne is a distressing problem for many adolescents. The physical changes of adolescence, especially the new secretion of hormones, proliferate cases of acne ranging from mild to severe. Some victims feel dirty, marred, or disfigured. If the parents harp on "bad diet" or lack of cleanliness as a cause, the situation worsens. Diet and cleanliness are secondary factors in acne; the primary cause is excessive glandular secretion. Teens need to know this is a normal condition in order to handle it well emotionally. They should be encouraged to watch their diets, but nagging and shaming them create more serious problems than a skin eruption.

Anxiety over physical looks is, of course, only one by-product of teen growth. The same growth that stirs feelings of awkwardness and inadequacy fuels conflicts about dependency and independence. Teenagers physically large enough to make it on their own begin asserting themselves and testing their newfound powers.

Dating problems and sexual questions also surface as a result of physical maturing. Although attitudes toward their bodies and sexuality have been gradually developing since the earliest years of life, teens are confronted for the first time with deeper realities and immense responsibilities of human sexuality. Adolescence also precipitates worry over one's vocational future and college education, and fears of failure take on a darker hue as physical, intellectual, and social growth propel the teen toward adulthood. So whatever problems our teenagers are facing, there is a strong likelihood that the physical-growth changes of adolescence play a prominent role. This is especially true of the next phase of adolescence we will consider—the awakening of our teenagers' sexuality.

3

Awakening Sexuality

One of the most puzzling experiences teenagers undergo is the awakening of their sexuality. Alternately exciting, mystifying, frightening, and confusing, the process of becoming aware of one's sexuality is a major task of adolescence. Some observers call it *the* task of adolescence.

From the first physical signs of puberty to the emotional and physical stress of one's "first love," teenagers go through a some-times-agonizing struggle with their sexuality. There may be storms of excitement, fear, guilt, anxiety, curiosity, embarrass-ment, or shame swirling around maturing sexuality. The per-plexed teen wonders if he is normal and assumes his problems must be worse than any of his friends'.

In its initial stages, awakening sexuality focuses on the physi-cal developments of adolescence and the so-called secondary sex characteristics, such as change of voice and growth of pubic hair. The changes evoke great interest, since they are "proofs" of emerging adulthood! Early development of these characteristics stirs a mixture of pride and fear.

The girl who matures physically before her agemates has the advantage of feeling more mature and enjoying attention not shared by her friends; but she may also be intimidated by the whistles, comments, and requests for dates by older admirers, and the sudden fuss over appropriate clothing by parents.

Ginny is a very physically mature fourteen-year-old. She put it this way, "Of course I like my body, but it also gets confusing. My girl friends are jealous or they tease me. Some of the boys just stare when I walk by, or make stupid comments. And my parents are panicked that I'll turn into a sex fiend or that some boy will 'take advantage of me.' I just wish people would let me be me!" Inside her adult-looking body, Ginny is still a young girl. And she knows this even though others may see her differently.

The boy that is physically strong and well developed also feels surging pride. His outward "maturity," however, may encourage

Early and Late Bloomers

him to rush ahead of his emotional maturity and involve him in situations beyond his experience to handle.

At this point, we should note that a teenager's feelings (or an adult's, for that matter) about his or her sexuality are not simply a reflection of physical attributes. In fact, the most important determinants of teenagers' feelings about their sexuality have been forged long before they reach physical sexuality maturity; for the relationship of a child in the first ten years of his life with his mother and father, and the parents' relationship with each other have shaped the fundamental features of the child's attitudes about himself, his sexual identity, and the opposite sex.

Boys, for example, need a good relationship with their fathers or father-substitutes, as a living model of what it is like to be a man. They also need a secure relationship with a loving and reasonably relaxed and happy mother in order to anticipate rewarding relationships with females. In much the same way, girls need mothers they trust and admire to make womanhood appealing. And they require sensitive and caring fathers, if marriage is to look attractive and the opposite sex appealing, rather than intimidating.

If these relationships have gone well in early years, it is likely that your teenager will adjust positively to his or her developing sexuality, no matter what the physical attributes may be. On the other hand, if your teenager has entered adolescence with strong reservations about his or her personal adequacy, or with negative feelings toward the opposite sex, crippling struggles with sexuality can result, even with superior physical endowments. The teen years bring new factors to the search for personal identity, but the new efforts are based on the successes and failures experienced in preceding years.

The beginning of the adolescent girl's menstrual cycle and the capacity of the adolescent boy to ejaculate semen are two more significant steps in the life of teenagers. Both experiences can stir a great deal of curiosity, anxiety, and guilt. If a teenage girl has been well prepared by her parents for the onset of menstruation, she will accept it as a healthy step in her development. She will realize that gestating babies get their food from mothers through the blood. She will understand that each month a small amount of blood collects in the uterus for the eventual start of a baby, and the absence of conception causes a release of the blood. Later she will learn how the menstrual cycle relates to conception and pregnancy.

Unfortunately, many parents have not felt sufficiently comfortable with their own sexuality to talk freely about their body functions and prepare their daughters emotionally for menstruation. Astonishing numbers of girls receive no explanation of even basic sexual functions. They meet the onset of menstruation with distress and confusion, wondering what is wrong and what, if anything, can be done to overcome this "problem." As one girl put it, "My mother talked about my period like the plague!"

Masturbation is an almost universal practice among teenage boys and, although the statistics are less complete, a common experience among teen girls. Approximately 90 percent of teenage boys surveyed acknowledge masturbating, at least occasionally. About half as many girls engage in masturbation, according to John Conger in *Contemporary Issues in Adolescent Development* (Harper & Row). This form of sexual experimentation can stimulate a great deal of anxiety and guilt, if the adolescent is unprepared. He wonders if masturbation is normal. He wonders if it is morally wrong. And he wonders what his parents would think or say if they knew about his secret activities. The cycle of stimulation, secrecy, fear, and guilt can become a real problem for the teenager who is already prone to excessive feelings of anxiety and guilt.

Sexually oriented jokes, girlie magazines, and recounting of sexual adventures appeal strongly to many adolescents, but innate modesty and anxiety toward the unknown cause a simultaneous hesitation. The conflict heightens for the Christian teenager with definite moral scruples. He yearns to satisfy his curiosity and to still live up to his ideals.

When parents have been factual and natural about their bodies, children's adaptation to sexual development will proceed smoothly. No undue curiosity about sex will dominate their minds, and a deep respect for their bodies will protect them from abusing this gift.

Following on the heels of puberty and masturbation is an expansion of the fantasy life of adolescents—especially in relation to one's acceptability by the opposite sex. Both boys and girls daydream about the individuals they would like to date, and about their own sexual adequacy and overall attractiveness with these people. Sometimes these fantasies become so persistent and repetitive that they too become the source of immense anxiety. The teenager begins to wonder if he or she is "obsessed by sex," and if his fantasy life is "normal."

Dating intensifies these sex-related conflicts. The social desire to be accepted and respected by members of the opposite sex merges with the physical desires of sexual and emotional intimacy to trigger a crucial struggle of the conscience. *How far should I go?* becomes a burning question in the minds of dating adolescents. Physical urges, curiosity, and desire for affection push for expression, but moral and spiritual convictions resist the pressure. The inner war is underway!

Overall maturity, self-respect, stable family relationships, and personal commitments to God will largely determine the outcome of this battle. They also determine the degree of guilt experienced and the sense of adequacy developed. An adolescent who feels unsure of his or her masculinity or femininity may be edged into premature sexual relationships to counteract self-doubts. And the adolescent who feels unloved and unaffirmed may seek solace from the opposite sex to find release from family conflicts and a temporary feeling of love and acceptability. This can be an especially tempting problem for a teenager being reared by a single parent and conscious of an emotional void.

The inescapable influence of our secular culture bombards teens with relativistic values, encouraging premarital sexual experiences. Several years ago a researcher found that 44 percent of boys and 30 percent of girls polled had sexual intercourse before they reached the age of sixteen. By the time they reached the age of nineteen, the frequency was up to 72 percent for boys and 57 percent for girls! One wonders if by now the percentage isn't even higher than that reported by Robert Sorensen in 1973! (*Adolescent Sexuality in Contemporary America: Personal Values and Sexual Behavior, Ages 13–19*, published by World Publishing).

This rampant loosening of sexual morality and its accompanying loss of respect for oneself and others make it imperative that concerned parents do all we can to help our offspring develop healthy sexual attitudes and solid moral and spiritual convictions. In chapter 17 we will consider some guidelines for helping teenagers through these intense struggles with their awakening sexuality.

4

Fluctuating Moods

Have you noticed your teenager shifting unexpectedly from one mood to another? One minute he is up and the next minute down. One day she is vivacious and the next morose. One day he is a gentleman and the next impossible. One day your daughter comes running into the house exclaiming, "Mom! I met the most terrific guy!" A few days later she angrily exclaims, "Don't ever mention that name around me again!" You shake your head and wonder what has happened. The answer: your teenager is on schedule!

Most teenagers have significant shifts of feelings and many show wide swings of mood. Some vacillate from elation to depression. One day they are on an emotional high: effervescent, joyful, and *thrilled* with life. The next day they look like their world has come to an end. They shuffle into the house from school and go directly to their rooms. In response to queries, they have nothing to say except, "Leave me alone!" or, "Nothing's wrong!" They mope around the house, doing nothing except making everybody else share their misery! Others shift rapidly from surprising politeness to ornery negativeness. Sometimes they sink into vocal hatred of someone—a special teacher or previous best friend who has offended them.

Joan, the mother of two teenage daughters, put it this way.

"Sometimes I just can't hardly cope with our youngest daughter. There are times when she is as sweet, warm, and loving as you could ever hope for. The next thing I know she is like an ice cube; she's defiant, hateful, and uncooperative."

Of course this unpredictability is hard for parents to take. If our teenagers are steadily happy and outgoing—or even consistently withdrawn and reticent—we can learn to adjust. We look for them to be happy or unhappy, quiet or active, cooperative or recalcitrant. But when we don't know from one day or moment to the next what to expect, it is difficult to get our bearings. We don't know whether to greet them cheerily or walk on eggshells at their appearance.

Roller-coaster changes of mood frustrate us "rational" adults, but an understanding of this phenomenon can help quiet our own reactions. The fundamental physical changes of teenage life do not influence only our teenagers' body size and shape, but their emotional stability and adjustment as well. The physical changes associated with puberty can upset one's entire psychic balance, and some teenagers go through rather lengthy periods of emotional upset. Time, maturity, and parental understanding usually help smooth out these peaks and valleys.

Teenage girls are often more subject to ups and downs than boys. The combination of innate physical differences and our cultural stereotyping, which represses male feelings, make adolescent mood swings more apparent in our daughters. This moodiness is sometimes compounded by hormonal changes experienced as a regular part of the menstrual cycle. Periodic moodiness, tearfulness, and hypersensitivity are often traceable to this bodily function.

In addition to these physical changes, your teenager is also learning to cope with new roles and responsibilities. Since our teenagers are now physically able to take care of themselves, people are expecting more of them. No longer must others cater to their needs. Adult habits must be learned. Approved driving skills must be developed. Responsibility for academic grades switches to the student, and discernment is expected in selecting friends.

Until adolescence, you have probably taken charge of most of these needs. You have seen that your young children were fed and clothed. You helped with homework when possible, or made sure it was done! You influenced the choice of friends by direct suggestion or prohibition. You provided transportation for varied events. But teenagers are increasingly free to make their own choices and demonstrate new responsibility. It is an exciting but perilous stretching.

If they reach out to a potential boyfriend or girl friend and are rebuffed, they cringe within. If they dent the family car, miss out on a prominent school position, or bring home an unexpectedly low grade, they may be devastated. Striving to please others, while forging new self-reliance, and trying to cope with wounded feelings, conflicts, illness, and guilty feelings, teens are understandably vulnerable to precipitous fluctuations in attitude and mood.

When we look at our teenagers' search for personal identity in a later chapter, we will see other causes of these unsettling emotional changes. For now, we will emphasize the importance of parental understanding of physical and social changes affecting emotional patterns in our adolescents. Everyone benefits when we parents learn to accept these temporary emotional swings and patiently and understandingly give our teenagers time to get their act together.

5

Peer Pressure

While I was working on this book, I asked a group of teenagers for some help. I wanted to hear firsthand some of their major concerns and the problems they face. Peer pressure was near the top of the list. Steve, a sixteen-year-old junior, put it this way. "Peer-group pressure is my hardest struggle. My friends want to do things that I know are unchristian, and it's hard not to go along. I guess this means my friends aren't good for me, but knowing that doesn't seem to make it easier. No one likes to be the oddball."

Few things strike more fear in the hearts of parents than the possibility of peer pressure. We look around at adolescents in our neighborhood or the local school—and quake inwardly at the sight. Some are hooked on fast cars and dangerous driving. A gang of slovenly youth hangs out at the local fast-food outlet. Some of the girls wear exceedingly seductive clothes, and others run around dropping a steady stream of profanity from their lips. Stories of wild parties abound, as well as those of drugs and violence on the high-school campus. Every gauge of teenage life seems to be declining.

Even more "normal" teenagers from so-called good families concern us. We wonder about their moral standards, their spiritual commitment, their political perspectives, their attitudes toward authority, and their responsibility—or lack of it. And we wonder about their music, their dress, and other current fads. In the face of all these disagreeable signs, we are tempted to brace ourselves for the worst.

Sometimes we can understand our teenagers better if we take a look at our own lives, and the way *we* respond to influence of our own peers. Look at the clothes we wear, the cars we drive, the houses we live in, and the foods we eat—chances are that we don't vary greatly from the norm! If narrow ties are out, we men don't want to be caught dead wearing one! And if long skirts are in, women want to be sure theirs are in style. If we parents are so strongly influenced by our peers, shouldn't we expect our teenagers to be sensitive to peer acceptance or rejection?

Our offsprings' urge to conform usually sharpens during the preteen and early teenage years. Their susceptibility to peer pressure then peaks around middle adolescence, and begins a gradual decline. This relatively predictable cycle tells us a great deal about the dynamics of peer pressure.

It begins its most rapid growth in early adolescence, when our children are for the first time moving out on their own and establishing their own identities. At this time they are loosening the ties of home, but do not yet have their inner resources sufficiently developed to take up the slack. For several years they will seek their identity in peer groups that offer sympathetic reinforcement for their struggle. To go against the group puts insecure teens in an emotional void. As they move into the later stages of adolescence, they find more confidence in their own abilities and decision-making powers. This growing sense of self-assurance enables them to learn to stand against the group and assert their individuality once again.

In spite of the potentially negative influence of peer pressure, the process behind it is entirely natural and God-given. Our teenagers are susceptible to their friends' influence, because they are in the process of weaning themselves from us and learning to think for themselves. For years they have grounded their identities in parental relationships. What we said and did was pretty much what they accepted as right or true or proper. But physical and intellectual growth incite independent action and thought. Part of the process of maturing is learning to think for oneself and being open to the influence of one's friends. In a sense, our teenagers are going from one form of dependency—*parental*—to another—*peer*—on their way to constructive self-reliance.

Now I realize the carbon-copy speech and dress and music of teenagers doesn't seem to be a great indication of individuality and thinking for oneself! In fact, the opposite seems true. But

from their perspective, our teenagers' temporary cookie-cutter conformity is an exercise in individuality—they are freeing themselves from the dependency of childhood!

As our teenagers turn away from us and try to find their own autonomy, they also feel a bit of isolation and loneliness. This is another cause of peer pressure. Their reaching out for independence gradually separates them emotionally from our parental love and support at the time they most need acceptance. Consequently, peers provide the needed approval and our teenagers may be willing to trade some of their values, ideals, and uniqueness to receive it.

Our teenagers' search for peer acceptance also stems partly from trying to find their place in a big, and potentially frightening world. In fact, this scary element gives peer influence much of its strength. After a dozen years of being a baby and a child, teenagers are suddenly thrust into a world where they must make their own choices and live out the consequences. They must learn to adapt to new people and accept responsibility. In the middle of all of these conflicting possibilities, where can they turn for help?

Parents are one potential source, and many teenagers feel the freedom to turn to us for guidance. But there are limitations in this direction. Since dependency is what the teenager is trying to put behind, turning back to one's parents may just reinforce the problem. Our teenagers can learn a great deal by identifying with others their own age and in similar circumstances. Although understanding parents still have the opportunity and capacity to aid this development, we must face the fact that we must give way to broader influences if our teenagers are ever to reach maturity. In chapter 15 we will look at several ways of maximizing the positive effect of peer influence and minimizing some potentially negative effects.

6

The Drive for Independence

Probably the single most important step from adolescence to maturity is the transition to healthy independence. For a dozen or so years, your preteenager has been largely dependent upon you. From the complete helplessness of infancy, he or she has learned to take more and more responsibility and increasing care for personal needs. He has learned to feed himself, read and write, and socialize with peers and adults. He has begun to master the king's English (though sometimes you wonder), and he can take care of himself in most ways physically. But until adolescence, your son or daughter has still been highly dependent upon you.

In addition to the obvious financial dependency, he has been dependent emotionally. He has looked to you for his sense of belonging, security, and confidence. When he was hurt, puzzled, or overwhelmed, he turned to you for support and guidance. And although he steadily gained a measure of self-sufficiency and came to rely increasingly on teachers and peers, he still has rooted the major portion of his identity in relationships with you.

During adolescence, all of this begins to change. Although parents leave a lasting imprint on their children's lives, a movement begins in the teenage years that eventually ends in leaving home, setting out on one's own, finding an autonomous sense of identity, and eventually establishing one's own family. This process usually does not take place without a bit of conflict and anxiety.

It is the rare person who moves from the dependency of childhood to the independence of adulthood without passing through stretches of troubled water on the way. Sometimes these conflicts are traumatic. An adolescent who believes the only way he can find his own identity is to totally reject his parents may run away from home, get married at an immature age, rebel against parental values, or in some way set up an adversary relationship with his parents. This is a tragic solution to a teenager's conflicting desires between dependency and independency. Yet it is one that many teenagers seem forced to take.

Have you noticed that sometimes your adolescents act a little like when they were only a couple of years of age? The typical two-year-old vacillates from almost helpless dependency to periods of total negativism and self-assertion. One moment they act like the helpless infants they were a few months earlier, and minutes later they are striving to show you they can do things on their own. Your teenagers are very likely going through much the same type of struggle at a more mature level.

Some days they are feeling confident about their ability to interact with their ever-enlarging world. They have close friends. They are doing fine at school. They are confident. And they have most things under control. Moments later their world is upside down. That same daughter that shrieked, "Leave me alone! I will make my own decisions!" comes to you in complete despair. "Mother!" she cries out, "What shall I do?" She is at a total loss. Suddenly she is overwhelmed with conflicts or decisions too big to handle.

Such extreme changes, or course, can be upsetting to parents. We wish they would make up their minds. If they want to be

adults, fine; they can accept responsibility and act that way. And if they have to be children, that's okay—*But, please,* we think, *Make up your mind!* The problem, of course, is that our teenagers are neither adults nor children.

They are adolescents who, in some ways, are still like children. They lack confidence, experience, and consistency, but they are also a lot like adults. Physically and intellectually they are near their peak. They can cope with a lot of stress and they can assume new challenges. Sometimes they have the tools, insights, and reserves to function very adultly. Other times they collapse. When they feel too inadequate, the only solution is to retreat to the security of childhood havens.

When a teenager (or person of any age, for that matter) gets in over his head and begins to feel overwhelmed, he tends to retreat to the methods he found successful for coping with stress in earlier years. Do you remember, for example, how your first child suffered a temporary regression after your second child was born? Most first children temporarily become a bit babylike at this time. If they have been weaned, they may want to go back to the bottle or the breast. And even though they can speak more maturely, they may resort to baby talk. Feeling threatened by the new adored arrival, they want to move back the clock to a time when things were going better! Or, if they sense this won't work, they may suddenly vault ahead, striving to mother their tiny sibling to increase their sense of importance.

When an adolescent encounters frustration, he frequently takes the same tack. If he has previously coped with conflict by running to Mother or Dad for support, he is likely to do the same. If he has become stubborn and pouted in a corner, he is likely to revert to that. And if he has given in and bemoaned his failure, he will probably repeat the act with just a moderate increase in intensity. All of these reactions are signs of your teenagers' conflicts between dependency and independency. They reflect healthy struggles to give up childish behavior, but also the fears of not being able to adapt to a massive, threatening world.

7

"I've Got to Find Myself"

One study of seven thousand high-school students, reported by Merton Strommen in *Five Cries of Youth* (Harper & Row), found that the single most troublesome concern for teenagers was the feeling of self-hatred! One of every five of these students reported severe problems with their self-esteem—and these were church youth! They reported feelings of failure, alienation, loneliness, lack of self-confidence, low self-regard and even thoughts of suicide! In short, they weren't satisfied with their own identity.

Most of the conflicts we have been discussing boil down to what we call the *adolescent identity crisis*. For a dozen years your teenager has been known as "the Smith boy," or "the Smith girl." Your child has looked up to you, literally and figuratively. When he was small and weak, you seemed like an omnipotent and omniscient god. As he grew and made comparisons, he concluded you were less than perfect, but you still were the most important adult in the world. "My dad can lick your dad!" was loyally believed, if not declared, throughout childhood. But somewhere along the way a new perspective forms. A budding teen wants to be known as Bill, or Susan, as the case may be, not as "the Smith boy," or "the Smith girl." Adolescent identity is flowering.

In the course of our advancing years, we all pass through a

number of identity crises. The first voluntary one comes at a year or two of age, when we gradually perceive ourselves as separate persons and start asserting our own wills. Another identity crisis comes with our first days of school; another with socially important junior-high and high-school years; another at marriage; another when we have young children; another when we again have the home to ourselves; and another when we adjust to retirement. Of them all, the most traumatic is the crisis of adolescence. In this stage we creep or we leap toward adult identity and stability.

For the person who has found his identity largely in his parents for a dozen years, this is not an easy process. *Our teenagers want to know who they are physically.* Their bodies are changing so rapidly, they aren't really acquainted with them. They want to

accelerate reaching physical potential, so they can assert their individuality. Will they be large or small, strong or lithe, attractive or plain?

Our teenagers want to know who they are sexually. They want to understand their newfound sexual desires. They want to know if they are acceptably masculine or feminine, as the case may be. And they want to unravel the implications of being a man or a woman in terms of future education, work, and marriage.

Teenagers also need to know who they are socially. They want to learn where they belong, and the people with whom they fit. Are they upper, lower, or middle class in taste, or can they move easily among people from a variety of social, cultural, and economic backgrounds? Our teenagers yearn to explore their relationships with us. Now that they are no longer children, they want to know how we evaluate them. Do we respect their ideas and encourage their desires for autonomy, or do we try to keep them as dependent as possible?

Our teenagers want to investigate their educational and vocational identity. What are they going to choose for a life's work? Is college for them? Will a trade or craft be more suitable? How does one uncover his best potential?

Deep down, *teenagers want to know their spiritual identity.* How do they approach their Creator? Are they acceptable to God, and how do they fit into God's plan for the universe? These are a few of the hundreds of identity questions flitting through the consciousness and subconscious of the normal teen. Above all else the teenager needs to settle the important question *Who am I?*

This is a momentous time for parents who are prepared to help their teenagers find a sense of individuality and autonomy. We can take great joy in seeing our children develop their unique gifts and potentialities. We can express pride in their accomplishments and we can experience a sense of fulfillment, as our sons and daughters progress toward readiness to have families of their own. But if we are not prepared, or if for one reason or another we strive to keep our children dependent on us, we make it difficult for them to traverse the paths from adolescence to adulthood.

Our teenagers' drive for independence and a sense of their own unique identity accounts for many of the conflicts we encounter with them. As long as our teenagers unquestioningly accept all of our pronouncements and choices, they are not developing their own individuality. They must form and express their own opinions to find their own identity. By nature, they start looking for areas of disagreement. Each difference of opinion is a chance to say, "I am unique and different from you. I am not just a copy of my parents."

I remember our son's first day in junior high. He came home and was more negative than he had been for ages. It was almost like he had read a book saying, "Now that you are in junior high you are supposed to be negative and argumentative!" He picked on his sister and tried to argue with nearly everything my wife and I had to say. I don't know if it's because he had a hard day, or if he was simply asserting his growing sense of personal identity, but whatever the cause, he was right on schedule! Kathy and I had to be very careful not to get sucked into his baited traps and to become sensitive to his inner needs and feelings.

This disagreeing, of course, is initially disconcerting. Our indignant reaction sets a vicious cycle in motion. Both we and our teenagers begin to look for opportunities to prove that we are right and the other is wrong. We want to let them know they aren't quite as intelligent as *they* think, and they want us to know that we aren't either! They become extremely dogmatic and believe they "know it all." Not until five or ten years later may these perceptions begin to change, as we both feel more secure in our own identity and less need to put each other down in order to bolster our own sagging self-esteem.

The compulsion to prove one is right, of course, can lead to relational disaster! To avoid getting caught in this trap, we must appreciate growth and encourage healthy formation of personal identity and autonomy. We must create opportunities for self-expression. And we must discuss issues with them in a flexible, nondogmatic way that esteems their opinions and perspectives.

Sometimes the drive for independence leads to spiritual rebellion. In attempting to free themselves from childish bonds and dependent relationships, our teenagers may develop a negative attitude toward God, the church, or spiritual commitments. Their family struggle generalizes to their relationship with their heavenly Father. Although disconcerting to parents, this is a very common phenomenon. Rather than panicking at signs of rebellion toward God and the church, we should renew our efforts to listen carefully to our teenagers' struggles and concerns and help them through these difficult times.

The search for a sense of personal identity is closely tied to our teenagers' need for a sense of self-respect. As they begin to form a comprehensive image of themselves, it is important that they see a person who is valued by others. One of the greatest contributions we can make to our teenagers' well-being is to demonstrate they are loved and esteemed. Helping them forge a positive concept of who they are is one of the central themes of the next seven chapters. There we will look at ways of communicating respect and worth, so our teenagers happily "find themselves."

Part II

Guidelines for Growth

8

Accept Your Teenager's Anxiety and Discontent

Rori is a seventeen-year-old high-school senior, who lives just down the block from our family. While I was working on this chapter, I decided to phone her to find out what her typical day was like. She happily agreed and quickly rattled off this schedule:

5:30–6:30	Out of bed, shower, breakfast, and so forth
6:30–7:30	Drill-team practice
7:41	Calculus
8:43	Typing
9:45	Choir
10:47	Psychology
11:35	Lunch
12:30	American Literature
1:30–3:25	Drill team
4:00	Arrive home
4:00–5:00	Homework
5:00–6:00	Dinner, chores, and so forth
6:00–9:00	Drill team
9:00–10:00	Home or drop by and see boyfriend at work
10:00	More homework or TV
11:00	Bed

Since I felt tired just listening to her hectic schedule, I asked Rori if she had this same schedule every day. "Oh, no," she said, "only three or four times a week. I use the other days to catch up on the homework I let go for drill team!" Then I suggested the second half of the year must be easier since drill-team practices would be over. "Yes," she replied, "it calms down a bit, but I'm also trying out for a lead in a musical that we will put on next spring!"

I thanked Rori for her help, hung up the phone, and breathed a sigh of relief! Then I wondered how many other adolescents have similarly hectic days. Few, of course, could outdo Rori, but many are under terrific pressure. Between their classwork, extracurricular activities, family responsibilities, and church functions life can be very busy.

We parents often look at childhood—including the years of adolescence—as kind of a lark, a happy-go-lucky time or a time of play. Teenagers, we reason, have few, if any, responsibilities. They have no living to earn, no children to rear, and no mortgage to pay. Consequently they are free to do essentially as they wish.

By contrast we have many responsibilities: obligations to children, to employers, to mates, to our churches, and a variety of other organizations and individuals. Since we are so busy with countless responsibilities, it is sometimes difficult to put ourselves in our teenagers' shoes. Instead we minimize our adolescents' conflicts and frustrations. We overlook their struggles. We regard their dating experiences as "puppy love," and in general we see adolescence as a playful interlude in life with few hardships and frustrations. That is a great distortion of the truth, as Rori's hectic schedule shows. Not only do our teenagers have busy schedules, but they often face very difficult decisions and perplexing problems.

As I work with groups of parents, I regularly ask these questions: "Would you say your teenage years were the happiest time

of your life?" and, "Would you say the teen years were the unhappiest time of your life?" Time after time I find that at least twice as many parents name the teen years as their most miserable time of life! As you think back on your adolescence, does it seem like one long stretch of emotional and familial bliss? Were you happy and contented throughout those years? Or were they painfully difficult at times?

Remember the anxiety you had over your first real date? If you are a father, you may recall the first time you asked a girl for a date. Perhaps you were too shy or embarrassed to ask her out face-to-face, so you resorted to the telephone. As you began to dial your pulse rate increased and your tongue tangled. You were really anxious and were praying that her father wouldn't answer the phone! At the other end of the line, your potential date may have been equally ill at ease, and when she said "yes", she tried not to sound overly eager.

When you went to pick her up, you made sure you looked just right. If it was a formal date, you ordered a corsage and wore a suit. Your parents checked you over before you left home. You rang the doorbell at your date's house and smothered an impulse to turn and run! Meeting her parents seemed like an adult torture device. Only gradually did you learn to relax and enjoy your date.

Perhaps your first date wasn't as traumatic as that but many adolescents' dates are. Fortunately teenagers today tend to "hang loose" a lot more about dating, but they still suffer a lot of anxiety over these experiences.

If your first date didn't rend your nerves, other new experiences probably did. You may have yearned to become a member of the drill team, the pom-pom girls, or the cheerleading squad. You practiced and practiced before the tryouts, performed well in the test, but didn't make the final cut, and were crushed at your failure. You went home in tears or turned to your friends for solace. It seemed that the world had ended. As you look back now, you wonder why you were so devastated, but at the time your disappointment was entirely real.

Perhaps you may have tried out for a school athletic team and failed to make the squad. Or if you did, it wasn't a lark. It was more like a battle. I can remember seeing most of a high-school football squad in tears after losing an important game. Needless to say their girl friends were in tears too!

These social and athletic Waterloos are only a few of our adolescents' frustrating experiences. Problems with teachers and grades, petty jealousies that split up friendships, and boy-girl tensions are likely to pop up anytime. And on top of all of these are difficulties getting along with brothers or sisters and mothers and dads. The possibilities for being overwhelmed with problems are almost endless. And these intensify the stresses of adapting to ever-changing body physique and the emotional oversensitivity that often comes with adolescence. We parents forget those years so easily!

Actually our teenagers may face more difficult decisions than you and I. Assuming that we have already selected a life's partner and are settled into our vocation and a relatively routine lifestyle, we can pretty well avoid many difficult decisions. Unfortunately our teenagers cannot do the same. When was the last time, for example, a friend tried to talk you into experimenting with drugs? When was the last time you had to struggle over how physically involved you would become on a date? And how long has it been since you had to decide where to attend college, who to marry, or what vocation to select?

While some of us go through stages where we reevaluate our marital, vocational, and moral choices, there is little doubt that our older adolescents are confronted much more frequently by these struggles than the typical parent. And they do not have the life experience and maturity we do, as they face these life-changing decisions! Before we jump to the conclusion that our teenagers' concerns and problems are minor or insignificant, we need to remind ourselves of all the momentous decisions they truly face!

In the middle of these potential frustrations and difficult decisions, our teenagers deeply need our sensitivity. If we minimize our sons' and daughters' struggles and problems, they feel misunderstood and alone. On top of their very real struggles, they will also have to cope with our lack of understanding. They often do this by feeling inept, abnormal, isolated, or alone. And teenagers don't need this kind of message. They feel different enough already!

To be explicit, this means *we should never minimize our teenagers' conflicts and frustrations.* If your son or daughter comes home shattered after breaking up with a boy or girl friend, don't casually advise: "There are plenty of other fish in the pond!" At the moment there is only one fish, and that one got away! Or if your daughter failed to make the drill team, don't evade the hurt by glibly consoling: "Oh, well, there are a lot of other good things that you can do." That may be true, but it is solace far removed from the pain.

Instead, give your teenager a chance to talk out his or her disappointment. Let them express their pent-up feelings. In fact, this kind of situation can give you one of your best opportunities for really communicating with your adolescents. If they know we are willing to listen and sympathize with their hurts, they will be willing to share with us at other times. But if we shut them off by minimizing their struggles, they will withdraw into themselves, clam up, or turn to one of their peers for understanding.

By not minimizing the seriousness of the tensions our teenagers face, we communicate a feeling of respect and understanding that goes a long way in enabling them to cope with these very problems. Our acceptance of their restlessness and discontent builds their freedom to accept themselves as they are, and gradually to find solutions to their problems. By taking them seriously, we let them know their concerns are genuine, and they needn't feel embarrassed, guilty, or odd because they are worried or upset.

Appreciating another person's anxiety and discontent is a skill that comes hard to many of us. Rather than empathizing, we tend to jump in with advice, as soon as we see someone in trouble. This response short-circuits the communication process. What is needed first is a caring ear. Think of your own experiences: when you are worried, discouraged, depressed, or angry, do you want someone to laugh away your feelings or correct your past actions? Of course not! You want someone to understand your feelings and echo your concern. Only after you feel fully understood are you ready for advice or new direction.

One good way of learning to accept another's anxieties and distress is to practice sensitive listening with your spouse or a good friend. Choose an issue that deeply concerns you and express your feelings about it in detail. Agree beforehand that the listener will make no suggestions at first, but will listen closely, not only to your words, but also to the feelings and meanings behind them. Then the listener will restate what he heard to express his support and understanding perception, and to allow opportunity for clarification and further elaboration. The exchange will help both participants listen more keenly and express their feelings more specifically. If clear communication fails, search for more descriptive terms, analogies, or symbols that will convey the feelings. For example, you may say, "I feel like I am in a dark pit"; or, "I am so frightened I could turn around and run."

When your deep concern has been thoroughly understood, reverse the roles of speaker and listener. But you may want to schedule that for another day! One major feeling at a time is all most of us can handle, and it can be mentally and emotionally taxing. After you have learned to understand and accept another person's feelings without being critical and to communicate your own, apply the new skill to building relationships with your teens. Listen empathetically without offering any advice. Just try to put yourself into their shoes and understand their feelings and emotions. This process is not the full scope of good communication, but it is an important starting place. It is also one of the most effective ways of helping our teenagers understand and express their emotions. This will aid them in learning to accept themselves in a threatening, changing world.

This process is called *active listening*. By that we mean a focused, compassionate attentiveness that will hear more than words and see further than the present moment. It's a grace that whispers, "I care," and helps give teenagers a real sense of being important people.

9

Never Argue With a Feeling

Since adolescence is a time of strong and varied emotional expression, we can expect our teenagers to experience intense emotions. Sometimes it is hostility, sometimes worry, sometimes hilarity, sometimes depression, and sometimes exalted awe! Whatever the emotion, nearly every teenager has periods of volcanic and fluctuating feelings.

When this happens many of us begin to get a little uptight ourselves. We like things on the status quo. A little self-expression spices up life, but if our sons or daughters become intensely emotional we want to quiet them down. If our daughter is enraged with a teacher or a friend she may hear our: "Now let's take it easy. No one's quite that bad." If she is perpetually worried over a boyfriend situation we tell her, "Relax," or, "Don't worry." And if she is discouraged or depressed we tell her, "Buck up. Everything is going to be okay."

These are nice-sounding phrases, and we may mean well. But, frankly, such sentiments do not help. In fact, they often make the situation worse. Imagine, for example, yourself feeling down and depressed. One thing after another has gone wrong and the end is not in sight. Along comes your mate or some friend who says, "Cheer up! There's a silver lining in every cloud!" Do you cheer up? Not likely! You're apt to be more exasperated or angry than

ever. The blithe words showed no understanding at all of the way you felt. If the person really understood and wanted to help, he would have silently respected your distress or said something like, "Rough day? Do you want to tell me about it?" This would have given you the opportunity of sharing exactly how you felt, and that is what you needed most.

Premature attempts to cheer another person usually reflect either our insensitivity to others or else our discomfort with the emotions they are feeling. In either case, we evade the awkwardness by trying to hurry upset teens out of their negative emotions.

On other occasions we may even try to argue our teenagers out of deep-running feelings. We give all kinds of reasons why they shouldn't feel lonely, mad, or fearful. We may even tell them their attitude is sinful and must be banished in a hurry. This tactic is destined to fail also.

Strong emotions do not yield to logic. Do you really think you can *talk* your sixteen-year-old out of love? The chances are she *fell* into it, and the only way she will get out is to *fall* right back out! And do you think you can convince your teenager not to be depressed or angry? Never! Even if your troubled teen is intellectually aware that his feelings are unrealistic, he can't change simply through reason, advice, or admonition.

Deep feelings are changed with understanding and acceptance. If your adolescent is riding a tide of negative emotion, the best way you can help him to solid ground is to jump in with him. Let him know you're nearby, being ready to listen when he feels like talking. And be careful not to squelch communication by quick judgment or slick solutions. There are times for parents to give teens direct guidance, but in the middle of a strong emotion is not one of them. It is impossible to take in advice when one is full of negative emotions. It is like trying to spit and swallow at the same time! It can't be done. Not until some of the strong emotions have been dissipated are teens ready to take in any new perspectives.

At this point some Christian parents protest, "I know my teenager needs my understanding. But what if his emotions are wrong or sinful? The Bible says we should 'put away our anger' and 'the fruit of the Spirit is joy'—not depression. Shouldn't we help them see how these attitudes are wrong?"

Yes, you definitely should. But the problem is how to do it. Most of us are well aware that negative emotions should be resolved. And Christians know that certain attitudes are downright sinful. But even a sinful attitude cannot be changed immediately. Our attitudes, habits, and emotions are the product of years of experiences and ingrained beliefs. To overcome them usually takes considerable time—along with a lot of understanding from

a caring person. That is why we should never argue with a
feeling.

No one has ever banished a deep feeling with an argument.
Feelings change with time, understanding, and new perspectives.
It is a process. When we allow our teenagers to express their
pent-up emotions, they can gradually begin to see things in another light. Open exposure helps them see there are, indeed,
"other fish in the pond" and that "the end of the world" hasn't
arrived. But it takes time and tender, loving care.

If you want to speed up the process, let your sons or daughters
know that you care about their feelings. If your son angrily says,
"That guy is such a mess," you will help him adjust by a sympathetic remark such as, "He really gets you down, doesn't he?" Or
a daughter who tearfully moans, "Oh, Mother!" will be encouraged by: "It happened, didn't it, honey?" She knows then
that you understand. In this way, you give teenagers permission
to acknowledge and deal with their painful emotions in the company of someone who cares. The simple words *I understand* will
never communicate your support as strongly as your open acceptance of a difficult emotion. Once we have sympathetically
said, "He really makes you angry!" or, "That must be very upsetting!" we don't need to tell them we understand. They already
know it. And because they do, they can start overcoming their
upsetting emotions, knowing they have an ally who will help, if
needed.

10

Be Sensitive to Sensitive Areas

When I was a sophomore in high school, a friend told me about his first experience shaving. For months he had been carefully checking his peach fuzz to see if he had grown enough to justify his first real shave. Finally the evidence seemed overwhelming, and he asked to borrow his father's electric razor. After a few joking remarks, his father gladly gave permission, and my friend proceeded with the great experiment. He took the shaver out of its box, plugged it in, and painstakingly attacked the whiskers. When he was finished, he wonderingly rubbed his face, looked in the mirror with new respect, and prided himself on his accomplishment. Immensely pleased with this leap toward adulthood, he dreamily began to put away the shaver—but just as he began to place it in the drawer, he took another look. Much to his chagrin, he noticed he had failed to remove the plastic cover over the blades before he started shaving!

You can imagine my friend's horror. After months (or even years) of looking forward to the day he would "become a man" he had dismally failed his puberty rites! Nothing could be worse! I am sure his father was quick to take full advantage of this little miscue, and he probably teased his son repeatedly. In fact, if I were to enter the home of my friend's parents today, I suspect

one of the first stories I would hear would be the one of Larry's first experience shaving!

This incident points to another area of caution in relating to our teenagers: we must learn to be sensitive to sensitive emotional areas. It is so easy to joke and poke fun at adolescents. They make great targets for teasing, because of their occasional physical or social awkwardness. They are going through a lot of new experiences and trying many things for the first time. We can joke about their height, their weight, their teeth braces, the size of their shoes, their funny friends, and on and on. But although it may be hilarious to us, it may be painful to our teens. Even if they laugh outwardly, our jokes are generally stirring up feelings of resentment or discomfort.

Each of the so-called little things we joke about can loom large to our teenagers. Being overweight is not funny. No girl enjoys being flat-chested and skinny as a rail. Everyone with braces on his teeth or pimples on his face wants to forget them! And early dating is tough enough without warding off parents' jokes. A sense of humor is a great attribute, but only if we can laugh at ourselves instead of others. In fact, when we poke fun at our teenagers, we are generally expressing our own anxieties and unresolved conflicts. A father who teases his son or daughter about his or her dating (or a girl or boyfriend) is generally, for example, expressing his own unconscious concern about his ability (or inability) to relate to the opposite sex. Chances are that when he was a teenager, he felt awkward and inadequate around girls. In those days he felt alternately curious, guilty, excited, and embarrassed about sex. Now, years later, he sees his son in the same quandary, and by making his son acutely aware of these struggles, the father gains a sense of superiority and adequacy. The only problem is the feeling is short-lived for the father and hurtful to the teenager. He is discouraged in developing natural relationships with girls, because the father is reinforcing his son's fears of inferiority.

Some parents attempt to motivate their children through sarcasm or ridicule. They believe teasing or pressuring teens about excess weight, untidiness, or poor grades will force positive changes. But these pressure tactics only create resentment and strong resistance.

Criticism has a similar effect. Sometimes we kid ourselves into thinking we are offering "constructive criticism." But most criticism is *not* constructive.

All of us respond better to encouragement and praise than to criticism. I often tell parents it takes ninety-nine compliments to make up for one criticism. I am not sure of the precise ratio, but I am sure teenagers need a lot more support and love and praise than criticism, in order to grow into responsible, productive adults.

One especially sensitive area for teenagers is their friends. Have you noticed how loyal teenagers are to their friends? Just say one negative sentence about them, and your son or daughter will quickly come to their defense. And if you continually ridicule them, you will stir up anger and risk cutting off communication.

You can imagine your own reaction to someone's jokes about your friends or your mate. Though you feel free to tease them a bit when just the two of you are together, there is no way you are going to let someone else make fun of them. The more someone jokes, the more you come to your friend's defense. And if they keep it up, you quickly become fed up with their sarcasm or teasing. Our adolescents respond the same way when we poke fun at *their* friends.

Teenagers also react strongly to our prejudices and biases against racial, political, social, or religious groups. Still idealistic and fair-minded in a cynical adult world, some teens can be terrific guides in spotting our own prejudices and biases. Perceptive teens pick up the signs a mile away, and if we are honest, we will often have to admit that they are right! This is one of many areas we can learn from our teens—if we are open to their understandings!

11

Be Reasonable, Dad! (And Mom)

Even though teenagers are nearing physical and intellectual maturity, they still need a good deal of parental guidance and support. This includes the setting of some specific limits and responsibilities for their best welfare. In the turmoil facing our teenagers, limits can become even more important. The rapid physical and social changes they experience tend to upset their whole psychic balance. Even sons and daughters who have been basically settled and well adjusted prior to the teen years may suddenly have difficulty adapting to new stresses. One result of these conflicts is the tendency to test all limits. The reasons for this are threefold.

To begin with, *healthy teenagers are looking for excitement.* They want to explore new things and test newfound freedoms. Fast or reckless driving, sexual experimentation, sampling of alcohol and drugs, and even mischievous vandalism have a certain appeal to most teenagers. Untried and risky activities lure the venturesome into sometimes dangerous diversions. They are looking for a thrill.

Another cause of teenagers' pressing all limits is *their actual physical and mental maturity.* No longer children, they expect to make a lot of choices on their own. They want to try out their developing capabilities by experimenting with things in the adult world. And what things are generally considered *adult*? Sex, alcohol, driving, and "being your own boss" are high on the list!

A third cause of teenagers' apparent rebellion is *a search for limits*. Although few teens would admit it, most feel periodically overwhelmed by their new opportunities and responsibilities. The new world is a bit frightening. Sometimes they would just as soon trade their newfound freedoms for a return to the time when parents made most of their decisions. Such dependency had its problems, but it was easier in a lot of ways!

What if he loses restraint and gets his girl friend pregnant? What if he succumbs to peer pressure and shoplifts merchandise in the felony category? These possibilities become actualities for millions of teens. But where were the parents?

It is just here that our teenagers need parental guidance and controls. They need to arrive home at a definite hour. They need to know we aren't going to let them have a heavy date at thirteen. And they need to know we have a genuine interest in their friends and the way they spend their time.

Eli was a responsible priest of Israel, but his sons were gluttonously taking meat that had been offered to God. They were also having sexual relations with women who gathered at the entrance of the tabernacle. Eli warned his sons that God would judge them, but they refused to listen. Later God told Eli the priesthood would be removed from his family because he didn't restrain them (1 Samuel 2:22–36). If God judged a leader of Israel for not restraining his young-adult sons, we should surely give serious attention to helping our teenagers manage their behavior!

Many parents tend toward one of the two extremes in setting limits for their teenagers. Some establish a large number of rigid rules, having arbitrarily decided how their teenagers are to act. They set the age for first dating. They severely restrict use of the car. They prohibit many social activities, and they have laid

down the law about church participation. In these and many other areas inflexible decisions have been made and authoritatively announced.

Other parents go to the opposite extreme. They conclude that since their teenagers are approaching adulthood, the practice of decision making can only be beneficial. If their thirteen-year-old daughter wants to date, they casually agree. If their fourteen-year-old son talks back to the schoolteacher, they call it "spunk." They assume it is their teenager's growing pains.

The biblical standard is somewhere between the extremes. It neither avoids our responsibility to guide and set limits—nor does it rigidly fix rules and requirements. The sensitive parent is aware of the cultural expectations and social pressures impinging on his adolescent sons and daughters. He knows his teenagers need to feel accepted by their peers and to learn increasingly to make their own decisions. Yet he recognizes they lack experience for new situations. Together they will talk over the need to be home at a decent hour. They will discuss their thirteen-year-old daughter's desires to date a seventeen-year-old. And they will discuss their sixteen-year-old son's desire to have a car of his own.

Wise parents will carefully listen to their teenagers' wishes and try to understand their perspectives. After a considerate hearing, they are ready to make a decision. Many times this can be a mutual decision. We can ask our teenagers what they think is a reasonable time to be in. We can find out more about the boy our girl desires to date, and the type of activities they intend to do. And based upon this information, we can come to an agreement. This is the ideal.

If we have talked over the matter and believe we should not go along with our teen's wish, we should share this conviction kindly—and be ready for some negative reaction. Anger is natural when one cannot have his way. Trying to force an artifical response would foment more trouble. A sense of security and appreciation for our concern will gradually develop in our teenagers, if our limits are reasonable, and we fairly consider issues with them.

Another way of taking the sting out of some of our prohibitions is to let teenagers know what they can look forward to. When will we allow our daughter to date? And when and under what conditions will we allow our son to have a car? If he saves up the money himself, will we let him buy one then? When he is seventeen, will we allow it? Just what are the conditions? This way teenagers don't begin to see life as a dead-end street with parents as policemen erratically waving stop signs and warning signals. They can begin to understand that we do want them to enjoy new privileges, as they are ready for them.

Carol and Don described two very different parental approaches to setting limits and guiding teens as they looked back a decade on their own experiences as adolescents. Carol recalled, "I remember how my mother used to make me feel like I was in prison, and she was the warden. There was no communication and no freedom for me to make decisions and mistakes of my own. It is hard for me even now to accept any authority or having people tell me what to do."

In contrast, Don recalled his parents' sensitivity to his needs for both freedom and guidance. He told me, "The most helpful thing my parents did to help my adolescence was to gradually give me my freedom and to trust me. I was not going to goof up my life and had no desire to do anything radical. My parents were wise enough to let me alone and not ride me too closely. If they had tried to hold too tightly, I might have done something stupid just to rebel!"

Since limit setting can provoke considerable conflict, consider these guidelines to help you choose the limits you will set for your teenagers.

1. *Recognize that every person is different.* What was right for you when you were a teen, or what is right for one teen is not necessarily suitable for another.

2. *Discuss the possible limits with your teenager before making a decision.* If your mind is already made up and you don't really listen to your son or daughter's perspective, he or she will know you are simply defending your position, rather than really looking at the situation with an open mind.

3. *Differentiate between a biblical absolute and your personal preference.* Sometimes we parents just naturally assume that our way of

looking at things is the biblical way. Whether it is hair length, clothing styles, or forms of entertainment, we conclude that we have the final word on the issue. Many teenagers have been turned off by parents who thought they were being helpful by claiming that certain forms of dress or certain social activities were obviously sinful and out of God's will. If we are convinced that a certain style of dress or an activity like movies or dancing is not helpful, we should tell our teenagers why we think so. And we can share with them our reasons. But we must take great care not to tell them the Bible clearly supports our position, unless God has in fact clearly spelled it out in Scripture. Our teens can read for themselves and are likely to be very resentful, when they start reading the Bible for themselves and find out we have been putting words in God's mouth!

4. *Be flexible.* There are reasonable exceptions to most rules. A special situation with proper safeguards may call for revised limits.

5. *Compare your standards to those of a variety of other parents.* This can help avoid narrow decisions. It can also help see where we may want to set limits that other parents haven't.

6. *Work toward cooperative development of standards.* Don't get in the position of being a policeman or a judge. You are a loving, caring parent, who wants to work together with your teenager for his good.

7. *Allow increased freedom and responsibility with age.* Sixteen-year-olds can generally make better decisions than they could at fourteen, and their responsible choices are encouraged by growing freedom to form decisions.

8. *Never set a limit without giving a good reason.* "Because I said so!" is a frustrating reason to growing, fair-minded teenagers. They are bright enough to understand our reasons even if they don't agree. We will develop their abilities to make decisions by giving a clear answer to their question *Why?*

A frequent temptation is to impose a rule or regulation to attempt to control teenagers *after* a problem has arisen. Let's say, for example, that you find out your teenage daughter has become involved in heavy petting or premarital sexual encounters. The immediate tendency is to find a rule or regulation that will limit this behavior. You might forbid her to date the offending boy, or set a very early curfew. Such limits are very unlikely to solve the problem. Premarital sexual experiences reflect a combination of forces including biological urges, desire for warmth, peer pressure, personal values, and family communication. None of these qualities are significantly affected by rules set up after a problem has arisen.

The need here is for improved parent-teen communication that will allow us to understand our teenager and her struggles, so that we can help her with the underlying problems. Rules and regulations are a cheap substitute for this type of understanding and are often imposed as a last-ditch sort of effort, when we think all else has failed. But instead of helping, they only stir up more resentment. Teenagers who are violating curfew, involved in premarital sex, or using drugs and alcohol are crying out for understanding. They are telling us they have a need and want us to understand and listen. To throw another rule at them in this situation is to give them one clear message. "We do not understand and we have given up being parents. All we know how to do now is try to control you like a warden does a prisoner."

This is certainly not to say that rules are unnecessary for our teens. The issue, however, is the sequence and the attitude. Before we establish any rule, we first take time to understand, to listen sympathetically, and to think through the issue, so that any decisions or regulations will grow out of a deep and sensitive caring for the welfare of each member of the family. In other words we should never attempt to establish rules apart from personal relationships. And if our relationships are so ruptured

that we cannot work out agreeable guidelines, we should probably look for a professional counselor, or a third party, who can
help us solve the underlying conflicts that are causing the heated
debates about behavior.

12

Yes, No, and Maybe So

Most parents have mixed feelings about their teenagers. We love them a great deal and have some confidence in their decision making. On the other hand we don't trust them entirely. We know they are human (like their parents!) and we also realize they lack the experience that can fortify them. When the crunch comes to letting them make weighty decisions, conscientious parents feel the pressure and sometimes give mixed signals. We would like to trust our teens but we aren't really sure we can. And out of our own anxiety we give mixed or conflicting messages.

We say, "I trust you, honey, but . . ." and everything after that three-letter qualification contradicts our affirmation of trust. Perhaps the question is a curfew hour on dating. We say, "I trust you, honey, but I think you should be home by ten-thirty." Or the issue may be the use of the family car. We say, "I trust you, son, but I just think you are a little young." In both cases we give mixed messages. In fact, we aren't telling the entire truth, because we haven't resolved the conflict in our own minds. A better way to handle this is to be honest and straightforward.

If we are worried when our daughter stays out past 10:30, we could say something such as, "I want to trust you, honey, but I also know and understand a lot about human nature." Or we

could say, "I would like to trust you, honey, but I am afraid the boy you are dating might be a little like your father was when we were dating!" Or we could say, "I know you have good intentions, honey, but I know how easy it is to get overly involved physically, when you stay out late." These comments accurately reflect your concerns without disparaging your daughter's character or giving contradictory messages. They also recognize human frailty, and the possibility that she will have some struggles, just like other girls her age.

If the issue is the family car, we might say something such as, "I think you are a responsible person, son, but I believe sixteen is too young an age to be driving a hundred miles at night. You're capable of doing it, and everything would probably go fine. But I would worry all night, and if anything did happen, I would feel terrible." Once again, we are being honest about our reservations, but we are careful not to impugn our teenager's capacity for trustworthiness—and in a way that honestly admits the problem may be our own excessive worry. You can also let him know that in another year you will be happy to let him make the trip.

This same principle applies to almost all communication with our teenagers. It is all too easy to give mixed messages. We say, "Have a good time." Then anxiously we add, "Get home as early as you can, because I won't be able to sleep until you return!" Our second directive essentially undoes the first. It says, "Have fun, but keep your mother on your mind too!" For an adolescent, that is hard to do!

Sometimes we respond to our teenagers' requests with garbled messages. We say, "It's up to you, honey. Do whatever you wish." But when she makes her decision, we caution: "Are you really *sure* that is what you want [or ought] to do?" First we said, "You are perfectly capable of making that decision." But when we heard it, we retracted our confidence. The teenager hears: "I really don't have the confidence that you have made the right decision. If you had chosen *my* way, I could trust you more."

Such second-guessing has one of two results. Some teenagers are angered by it. They sit up and say, "If you don't want me to make my own decision, then say so!" Others are baffled, and either give in meekly or carry out their decision under a cloud of doubt or fear. Both of these responses undermine their developing ability to make responsible decisions and live with the consequences.

The best way to avoid mixed messages is to give either a definite prohibition, an unqualified permission, or an open choice. In other words we should say *yes*, *no*, or, "It's up to you." When we tell our teenagers it is up to them, we should *leave* it to them and support them in their decision and the outcome. Never make de-

cision making a fearful event by second-guessing unpleasant results with the mournful: "I wondered all along if it was the right
thing to do!"

Sensitivity to our tendency to give mixed messages can help
our relationship with our teenagers in another way. By recogniz-
ing that our mixed messages stem from our own anxieties and
our own past temptations and failures, we are encouraged to talk
them over calmly with our adolescents. This helps build better
communication. If we honestly (but unsensationally) tell our
children how we used to drive, how we struggled with sexual
feelings, or how we pulled some stupid pranks, they can see that
we do not consider ourselves superior to them. In admitting our
own hang-ups, we are less likely to imply a harsh condemnation
of our teenagers for wanting to drive fast, explore sexually, or try
some exciting prank or activity. Shared feelings give us a better
basis for mutual understanding, and it also helps our teenagers
accept the limits and guidance we give them.

13

Let's Be Friends

We have been describing our teenagers' growth and changes at considerable length. These changes, however, are only one side of the coin. If our relationship with our teenagers is going to be harmonious, we must be changing too! We parents have our own identity crises and our own developmental stages.

Some of us make excellent parents for young infants. We are patient, kind, and loving, and find it easy to care for a helpless baby. And some of us do a terrific job during the children's pre-school and elementary years. As long as our children are relatively dependent and tend to follow our instructions, we get along quite well. But once they hit the junior-high or high-school level, we start having problems. We are used to telling them what to do and having them obey. We are used to caring for many of their needs. And we are used to spending time together as a family. Now all of that begins to change. Our teenagers start thinking for themselves. They start caring for their own needs. And they make new friends and have less and less time at home. If we are not careful, we will continue to parent them the way we did when they were younger, and this can cause serious problems.

Recall your relationship with your own parents. If you are like most "modern Americans," you do not live near them now. You probably manage to see them periodically. In any case, the chances are that you have developed a very different kind of relationship with your parents than the one you had while in their home. If your parents are still living, your relationship is probably more like peers or friends than parent-child. While they may occasionally try to exert a parental prerogative to worry over you or offer some advice, by and large you see them as good friends. You respect your parents and will always have a special relationship with them, but the former notions of authority and dependency have vanished, because you are an adult too.

One way of helping our teenagers grow toward maturity is to allow this type of change to gradually come in to our relationship with them. During our offspring's adolescence, we should increasingly move away from the role of authority and control toward a relationship of "peerness" and friendship. Here is the way one father expressed this need in writing to his twenty-year-old son during a seminar in family communication:

Dear Son,

I realized something the other day that I would like to share with you. I became aware of how much we had missed during the years when you were a teenager and growing up at home. I remembered how awkward it was to talk with you, and how when we did talk, it only seemed superficial, never in depth. I never asked you what was on your mind, how you felt about something, or what your opinion was. And I shared my thoughts with you only when it was necessary or forced.

I think I failed to consider what you were going through at the time in your life. I guess I figured you would just grow up and learn things naturally, and I would only step in to keep you out of trouble.

How I wish now that we had shared our thoughts together more often—just opened our hearts to each other, not worrying that we were father and son, but not forgetting that either. I hope the next time we are together, we can share more with each other and make up for some lost time. Perhaps it's never too late.

Love,

YOUR DAD

This father saw—perhaps just in the nick of time—that he needed to be friends with his son.

Ideally, our children have seen us as their friends for years. But if they haven't—if we have been parents at the expense of being friends—it is time to make the change! We need to learn to be their buddies or companions. We need to learn to enjoy each other. We need to play ball together, shop together, laugh together, and in many little ways find times to be together.

When this kind of relationship is lacking, the only solid contact we have is when we have a problem—when we are at the dinner table, or when we are facing something serious together. Consequently our teenagers learn to see us as distant or uninvolved, or they see us as only interested when there is a chore to do, a church service to attend, or a warning to be issued.

On the other hand, if we learn to genuinely enjoy our children and be friends with them, we help them make the transition to adulthood, and we gain a platform for our counsel and direction. In essence, we earn the right to lead, counsel, and discipline our teenagers by being their friends, as well as their parents. We build an affectionate bond that makes them want to listen and to value what we say. And we reduce the potential friction and resentment when we do set limits on their actions.

This point can be easily misunderstood, as there are two disastrous things that can be mistaken for the type of relationship I am suggesting. First, I am not suggesting you give up your role as

a parent and abdicate your parental responsibilities. As long as your offspring are in their adolescent years, they will continue to need your God-assigned guidance, support, and limits. The other procedure I am not suggesting is that you try to act like you are a teenager too! Some parents unwisely attempt to be "one of the gang." They jump into the middle of their teenagers' parties, dress and act younger than their age, and in general try to relive their own adolescence. But we cannot be "one of the gang," and our teenagers will cringe at our awkward attempt. We are grown adults, and our teenagers want us to "act our age." Teens don't want us to continue treating them like children; neither do they want us to try to be one of the gang. When I asked Sharon, a fourteen-year-old freshman, the best thing about her relationship with her parents she replied, "My parents can easily relate to teenage kids but still don't try to act too buddy-buddy with my friends. They keep their parent ways and suggestions." Like Sharon, most teenagers want us to "keep our parent ways," as long as we are sensitive and kind. They have plenty of peer relationships, and they need something else from us. A good adult friend who can listen sympathetically, offer counsel, and set prudent limits is valuable to them. They also want to enjoy our times together and to have some deeply enriching moments as a family.

One of the best ways to do this is to take an interest in our teenagers' activities. If they are into sports, we should share these pursuits. We should attend their games and get involved as much as possible. Hobbies or church activities offer other opportunities to share new experiences and insights. We should show an interest and offer to help in any way we can. The possibilities are endless, but the principle is very simple. To maintain a good relationship with our teenagers, we must share their interests and spend time with them. We should not intrude where we are not wanted, but we should express a sincere interest in the things they enjoy. Rewarding friendships are waiting in your own family.

14

Fragile Egos: Handle With Respect

Sheri, a young woman in her twenties, wrote me a long letter when I asked her to describe the most difficult experience she faced as a teenager. Here is part of her answer:

> The thing I remember about being a teenager was the feeling of being a cork on the open sea. Things would upset me so deeply that I actually drove myself into depression. I wanted someone to say, "It is hard being a teen"; or, "I understand." I needed someone who remembered how it was. I needed someone to give me honest answers, not just to use my questions as an opening for a preaching session.
>
> When you are in high school, you want to feel needed. Teachers tell you what to do; the family tells you what to do; and your friends tell you what to do. Doesn't anyone need me for more than a puppet, to make me do what they want me to do?

Sheri was crying out to be understood, accepted, and respected. She wanted to be acknowledged as an individual.

More than almost anything else, our teenagers want our respect. In their struggle for maturity, they need parents to value their ideas and listen to their opinions. They are stung by comments such as, "You're too young"; or, "It's none of your business"; or, "You'll understand when you get older." Each of these remarks implies that our teenagers are too immature or irresponsible to consider serious subjects, and resentment and rebellion are the likely results.

Probably the single best way to communicate respect to our teenagers is to learn to listen. We tend to think of communication as telling someone something. As parents, *we* want to get *our* message across to our sons and daughters. *We* want to let *them* know what is expected. And *we* want to be sure they know what *they* should do. This is *talking*—but it is not *communication*. Communication is both sending *and* receiving a message, and it usually begins with our willingness to hear before we speak.

Let's face it: many parents haven't the foggiest notion of what is going on in their teenagers' minds. We are well aware of their behavior and we see some attitudes that we appreciate—and some we would like to change. But as far as understanding the inner world of our teenagers' minds and emotions, we are essentially strangers. We might as well be trying to find a pin in a dark closet or see through a solid wall. If we've made some feeble efforts to penetrate the outer shell, we may have found our teenagers aren't prepared to let us in. The reason is they don't fully trust our motives. They are afraid we want to know more, so we can judge or correct or trample on their feelings and ideas.

Sandy put it this way: "Maybe I can share how it's hard for a teen with parents. I'm eighteen now and can look back over the years and see where I wish things could have been different. For one thing, I wish my parents would have been more open and able to share. Everytime I want to express my feelings about something, I'm quickly shut up, but I sure do have to hear *their* feelings on the matter. I also wish my mother, especially, but sometimes my father, could have been more understanding. There are a lot of things that I would have loved to share with my mother but couldn't and still can't, because I would have been condemned. I guess what I'm saying is that my parents were never my friends."

One way of breaking this impasse is to pause and ponder whether we really *want* to understand our teenagers. Teenagers have all sorts of fascinating ideas and complex feelings. They are intricate people with kaleidoscopic interests and can be great fun to know! And most important of all, they desperately need our understanding. One of the greatest mistakes a parent can make is to underestimate his offspring's need for our time and love and understanding.

Although we cannot dissect our adolescents' brains, we can learn to see what is happening in their minds. As we learn to listen and to value their ideas, they will reveal more and more what is going on inside. As they see they can trust us with their feelings, they will dare to share more of their inner selves. Cheryl, now a young mother herself, put it this way. "When I was going through my teenage years, the biggest thing that I looked for was someone to talk to who would really listen and not just talk *at* me!"

Closely related to the ability to listen is the willingness to be honest about own attitudes and actions. Most of us spend a lot of time puzzling over what our teenagers are thinking or doing, but little time in sharing our own experiences. And we spend notoriously more time focusing on their faults and failures than on our own! But the Bible says we are to confess our faults one to another (James 5:16). And that we are to bear each other's burdens (Galatians 6:2). If I understand these passages correctly, they mean that both parties should share their faults and burdens, not just one. They mean that we, as parents, should be willing to let our children know that we make mistakes. And that we should ask forgiveness when we have wronged them. This helps us work together on building more harmonious relationships in the future.

To be specific, this may mean we need to admit that we are a little rigid or narrow-minded, or that we worry unduly about our teens. We may have to admit that we haven't thought through the reasons for some of our regulations. We may have to confess we have been wrong in correcting them in anger. And we may have to declare we have been too busy to spend the necessary time to really understand their feelings and perspectives. None of this means that we are failures. It simply means that we recognize we are imperfect parents and we are sensible enough to admit it, even to our children. When we display the freedom to acknowledge our weaknesses and failures, it is much easier for our teenagers to do the same. No longer will we engage in a perpetual contest to see who is right, or to defend our position. Instead, we can learn to value each other more deeply and communicate respect.

Sometimes we unthinkingly communicate disrespect to our teenagers by the patronizing way we talk to them, or by the nicknames or labels we attach. We say, "What's the matter with you, anyway!" in a tone that indicates we think they are stupid, recalcitrant, or wicked; we use derogatory terms such as *lazy*, *fat*, or *dumb*.

At one meeting I led for parents, I asked the people to share a few of the nicknames or other designations their parents applied to them. The response included: *Stupid, Skinny, Scatterbrain, Grasshopper Brain, Crisco* (as in *Fat Can*), *Clumsy, Slowpoke, Fat Cow's Tail.* One woman broke into tears when she recalled that her father used to call her *Devil Daughter!* Another time a man said his parents used to call him "Chief Wetum Pants—of the Pee Pee tribe"!

Some of these epithets are funny and some are tragic but they all tend to disparage the children. These labels sometimes be-

come ingrained in children's personalities and form part of their self-image. Children who have been labeled *stupid* may feel mentally inferior, even after they gain a college degree.

The process of labeling also elevates one person above another. It puts the judge on a pedestal, where he can pronounce judgment on others. This is most unfortunate since it estranges people from one another. Rarely does it effect change in behavior or ameliorate a problem.

It is strange that we know how these verbal arrows hurt, yet we shoot them at our sensitive children. If we want to build up our teenagers' self-esteem and earn their respect and admiration, we must learn to stop resorting to this type of character assassination.

Another way of showing respect for our children is to involve them in family decision making. From the time our children are very young, we should begin preparing them to make decisions on their own. By the time they are in their teen years, they should be practiced in the process of evaluating options and making good choices. They should have a voice in most decisions in our families. Whether it be the type of car we are about to buy, the choice of a vacation spot, the color of the new carpet, or where we are going out for dinner, our teenagers' opinions should be asked and valued.

Take vacations, for example. If your family is like most, you and your spouse sit down and decide where you will spend your vacation and call in the kids and break the news. "Guess what!" you announce. "We have decided to go visit Uncle John and Aunt Mary for vacation this summer." "Oh, no! Do we have to?" the kids reply. And then we set about trying to convince them they will have a great time visiting Uncle John and Aunt Mary. Unfortunately we all know it is not what they will really enjoy doing.

How much better to sit down as a family and make our plans together. Maybe the kids would like to go to the beach (or the mountains), and we can work out a compromise. How about visiting Uncle John and Aunt Mary this year and going to the beach next summer? Or how about spending one week with Uncle John and Aunt Mary and one week at the beach? Or how about being really creative and meeting Uncle John and Aunt Mary at the beach? Our teenagers need vacations, too, and there is every likelihood that we can come to a mutually satisfying decision.

This doesn't mean that our teenagers make all the decisions. It simply means that we ask for their ideas, and that we discuss things as a family, and try to take everyone's feelings into consideration. Sometimes we may decide to go with our children's wishes, even though that wasn't our first choice. Other times we will listen, consider, and decide on another option. In either case, our desire to seek their perspectives and bring them into our family planning communicates a sense of respect that they will always cherish. It also sets an example for their activities in their relation to us. Again, by giving we gain.

Part III

Common Conflicts

15

Coping With Peer Pressure

In chapter 5 we considered some of the dynamics of peer pressure. We saw that it is a normal phenomenon, influenced by our teenagers' needs for love and acceptance and their desires to begin breaking the ties of childhood and finding new sources of support. Now we will look at specific guidelines for helping our teenagers benefit from, rather than be harmed by their peer relationships.

The starting place is to realize peer influences do not have to be negative and harmful. A proverb says, "He who walks with the wise grows wise, but a companion of fools suffers harm" (13:20). Many teenagers are helped immensely by their friends, and all learn some important lessons in interacting with their peers. Recently the teenage son of some acquaintances of ours came home from a party, drunk. It was the first time this had happened, and the parents were shocked. To their surprise, a few days later, they discovered that their son's teenage friends had already talked straight with him about the harm he could suffer if he continued drinking!

During adolescence, our teenagers try out new social roles. They are learning what it is like to choose friends and build relationships. These skills are essential in later life, and adolescence is the place to learn them. Without growing experiences in adolescence, our children will enter marriage and other adult relationships seriously deficient.

Sometimes our teenagers' friends can help them overcome potentially serious problems. They hear out our troubled offspring when we are too busy or otherwise are unable to listen. Sympathetically they encourage and even offer wise guidance. Sometimes our teenagers' peer relationships help correct or overcome negative attitudes they have learned from us. A teenage girl, whose father is a hard-driving, demanding and perfectionistic person, for example, may be under constant pressure to perform in order to gain her father's approval. A good relationship with a boyfriend may for the first time give her a glimpse of the fact that she can be accepted exactly as she is.

A teenage boy, whose mother has been controlling or overprotective, may have a distorted image of all women. A healthy relationship with a girl friend may help him see it is possible to relate to the opposite sex in an open, mutually rewarding manner. He can begin to alter his perception that all women are controlling, and he can begin to feel more at ease and less threatened when with the opposite sex. These changes will serve him well when he marries.

Even in families whith good relationships, adolescents need peer friendships for the give-and-take between "equals" that is critical for normal growth. For these reasons, *we need to affirm the value of our adolescents' friends and encourage our teenagers to bring their friends to our house or to have them "drop by" for visits.* Parents who know and like their adolescents' friends, and are comfortable having them around, are much less likely to have problems with negative peer influence.

One parent offered this advice: "Be prepared for an ever-changing cast of characters—friends of all sizes, talents, and dispositions. One by one they will file through your home and your

life. Their ultimate destination will be your heart and your refrigerator!"

By being hospitable to our son's and daughter's friends, we are demonstrating the value of friendships. We are also avoiding much anxiety that accompanies our teens' associations with friends little known to us. One of the main reasons we are so afraid of negative peer influence is that we generally don't know much about the people our teens are running with. We get an outward glance or a quick impression, but we seldom take time to sit and chat and really get acquainted.

Hopefully, we have started valuing our children's friends long before they reach the age of adolescence. If not, we need to make up for lost time. We can open our home for a party. We can

bring out a snack when friends drop by. We can invite a friend
for a weekend visit. We can pay a friend's way to a parent-teen
outing or give a welcome to a family activity. There are endless
ways of cultivating our teen's friends and of working out enjoyable times together.

These attentions tell our teenagers that they and their friends
are important to us, and that helps make us more important to
them. Encouraged by our acceptance, our teens will be more inclined to be discriminating in their choice of friends.

Attitudes toward our teenager's friends are as important as our actions.
Teenagers tend to be intensely loyal. To disparage a friend is to
insult your teen. We should think twice before we dispense criti-
cisms of our adolescents' friends. Even when we have some serious questions about our adolescents' friends, it is best to refrain
from criticism. Instead, we can ask our adolescents how *they* feel
about the friend in question. Quite often you will find your son
or daughter has some of the same reservations you do. If we take
time to listen and don't jump in too soon, we may find that they
are pretty good judges of character themselves!

If our teenagers don't perceive some potential problem that we
observe, we can raise our concern in a nonjudgmental way. We
might say, "What do you think about Tom's drinking?" Or "I
wonder why Tom has trouble getting along with his teachers?"
These questions or other concerned comments express concern
over Tom's well-being. They also encourage discussion that is
instantly cancelled by accusatory statements like: "I don't want
you running around with that alcoholic!" or, "Your friend has a
terrible attitude!"

*If our teenagers join the wrong crowd, or we sense they are headed for
trouble because of the friends they keep, we need to explore the underlying
causes.* Chances are we won't have to search far. The single most
important reason children from "good families" choose the
wrong crowd is the lack of a warm and sustaining relationship at

home. In fact, psychological research indicates the lack of family unity and communication is one of the three major causes of susceptibility to negative peer pressure. The other two are low self-esteem and the presence of a very strong and homogeneous peer pressure. Sometimes we fathers are just too busy to spend a lot of time with our adolescents. We leave early for work and come home late. By the time they finish supper, someone is off to another activity or meeting that shrinks family time together and divides interests. When this is the case, we had better reevaluate work and family priorities. Too many families are becoming strangers to one another from lack of quality time together.

I am one of those parents who had to learn to relax and enjoy my family. I grew up on a small farm in Arizona, where a high value was accorded to hard work, and little time given to family play. After our own children were born, I began to realize I was following the same pattern with our children. I was among the first to arrive at work and one of the last to leave. I arrived home tired and didn't feel like playing with the kids. Gradually I began to realize Dickie and Debbie needed more of my time—and that I needed to learn to relax and enjoy them! I had to face the fact that it was easier writing about rearing children than doing it! And I had to admit that I was a workaholic and would neglect my family, if I wasn't careful! As I changed my schedule and spent more time with my children, I began to learn the meaning of fatherhood. We played games, surfed, shopped, and did all kinds of enjoyable things. My kids showed me I had been missing a lot of living.

If you are a bit this way, let me encourage you to step up your family fun. Go to your teens' athletic contest this week. Take your son fishing, biking, or skiing. Work on his car together. Have a lunch date with your daughter, or go window shopping. The "right" activities are not as important as the doing. Learn how to enjoy your adolescents. If they are happy with you and your spouse, they will not seek out undesirable companions to make up for lack of love and approval at home.

Another suggestion for coping with the possible negative effect of peer pressure is to *see that we attend a church that has a youth group that appeals to our teenagers.* We may need to seriously consider changing churches, so our teenagers will have an opportunity to fellowship with Christian young people they enjoy and serve in challenging ministries. We will look further at this possibility in chapter 20. Here I simply want to point out that one reason for church attendance is personal encouragement, and it is hard for a teenager to be encouraged by a group of adolescents he finds incompatible, or among adults who seem out of touch with teenagers. The author of Hebrews tells Christians to "encourage one another daily, as long as it is called Today, so that none of you may be hardened by sin's deceitfulness" (3:13). Support by Christian friends helps us avoid sin. If we want to help our teenagers avoid sin, fellowship with encouraging friends should be a high priority.

Sometimes teenagers turn excessively to their friends, because they feel overprotected or restrained at home. If we supervise details and regularly impose our decisions, they instinctively retreat toward breathing space. Like us, they want freedom from pressure, coercion, and criticism, and they know it's available with their friends.

Other times teens turn to questionable peers with their problems instead of to parents because of low self-esteem. Most of us choose friends that match the mental picture we have of ourselves. If this is a probelm with our teens, we may need to seek skilled professional help. We may need assistance in overcoming some destructive parental habits and in building up our adolescents' sense of self-esteem and self-reliance.

Ask yourself what your teenagers' friends reveal about their relationship with you. Do their choices reflect an acceptance of you and your values? Do they reflect hidden (or not so hidden) resentments? Are there signs of self-rejection in undesirable choices of friends? Or are the signs largely positive? As we understand the meanings of our adolescents' choices of friends, we are in a position to influence them constructively in further growth.

16

Dating

"I still remember the time Kari burst out in tears, just because I asked her if she had a date that night. Little did I realize that she was heartbroken, because no one asked her out." These words, spoken by the father of a twenty-year-old girl reflect the great anxiety teenagers often have over dating. In fact the study of teenagers by Merton Strommen in *Five Cries of Youth* found that 51 percent of the adolescents spent some time every day, thinking about how to keep members of the opposite sex interested in them.

The anxiety our teenagers have over their ability to relate to the opposite sex is frequently matched only by our parental anxiety over these same relationships! We seem to go through the same fears and anticipations that our teenagers do about dating, plus a few of our own. We want our teenagers to have good dating experiences, to be liked by the opposite sex, and to have a variety of dating experiences. We don't want them to feel inadequate, left out, odd, or unacceptable. And we don't want them to become too involved physically or emotionally. With all of these concerns, it is natural that we do not always find it easy to calmly guide our teenagers through their dating experiences.

Some parents, especially mothers, are so anxious for their teenagers to have dates that they begin to encourage them in their junior-high-school years. They give "hints" about boys they think are "nice" or "likeable," and in a variety of ways interject themselves into their daughter's dating; or they try to teach them how to act so they can "keep" their boyfriends. This, of course, is not healthy.

For some reason this type of mother has apparently not come to grips with her own sexual adjustment. Perhaps she didn't have as many dating opportunities as she wanted when she was a teenager. Perhaps she never outgrew her adolescent fixation with "romance." Or perhaps she is so attached to her daughter that she is unable to allow the girl to act on her own. She seeks to bind her daughter to herself by attempting to manage and vicariously experience her daughter's dating experiences.

Other parents are overly anxious about their teenagers' potential physical intimacies. Perhaps recalling their own struggles in this area, they worry excessively, especially over the boys their first daughter dates. They want to be sure no one takes advantage of their "innocent" daughter. Some parents are almost fanatical about this. They refuse to let their daughters date until a late age, suspiciously scrutinize even casual dates, set an early—and often unreasonable—curfew time, and wait for their daughter's return like police inspectors. Dating begins to look like a crime!

Although it is important to be concerned about our teenagers' dating, and although parents can be of help to them in many ways, this fearful aversion is more the parent's problem than the daughter's. Typically, parents with extremely strict attitudes have had to struggle (and sometimes not too successfully) with their own sexuality. They either let things get out of hand when they were teenagers, or they felt it necessary to avoid physical contact with the opposite sex like the plague in order to keep their sexual urges under control.

If we are a bit this way, we may have to be careful not to impose our own neurotic controls on our teenagers and to be sensi-

tive to their own strengths and weaknesses, rather than on our own. We will need to remember that dating can be a very positive experience. It doesn't have to be fraught with problems.

Our teenagers need opportunities to extend their friendships beyond our family's boundaries and beyond friends of the same sex. This is a healthy part of growing up and preparing for selection of a life mate. Many adults can look back on teenage dating with good memories. We made many friends, broadened our interests, developed our personalities, and had happy times. Some of us had steady dating experiences that gave a sense of stability and belonging that we didn't have at home. And even though we suffered when we "broke up" the relationship, we were better prepared for the next friendship. As parents, we should remember these times and look forward to good experiences for our adolescents.

Before we consider some of the problems of teenage dating and specific suggestions for parental guidance, let's look at some general contributions we can make to our teenagers' dating experiences. Since dating is both a new form of interpersonal relationship and an exercise of new social skills, we can offer practical instruction they will find useful. Though some teenagers want to find their own way, others will appreciate suggestions from those who have already walked the trail. A good time to begin is at the beginning with the first date.

A casual conversation can introduce the subject of asking a girl for a date. We can let our son know that he should not ask a potential date, "What are you doing Saturday night?" or, "Are you free Saturday evening?" His purpose is not to pry into what she is doing Saturday night! The question should be direct: "Would you like to go to _____ with me on Saturday evening?" This gives opportunity to say an honest *no* or *yes*. It avoids putting her in an awkward spot and may avoid unwanted embarrassment for your son!

Instructions on other courtesies, such as going to the door to meet a date, politely greeting the parents, telling them what time he will return with their daughter, and opening the car door for his companion will go a long way to start dating off pleasantly. Such actions instill confidence in both the girl and her parents for the outing.

A discussion about money on dates can also be helpful. I remember a few years ago when our son Dickie, then eleven, took me out for a birthday dinner. Since it was Dickie's treat, I suggested that he telephone for the reservations. With a little coaching, he made the arrangements, including asking for a window table! When we arrived at the restaurant, I stayed in the background and let Dickie talk to the maitre d'. At first the head waiter talked past Dickie to me, but I ignored him and let Dickie do the talking. As we were being seated, I told him I was Dickie's guest.

As Dickie and I studied the menu, he asked me what I wanted. Feeling a bit like a date who doesn't know how expensive a meal to order, I decided to take the opportunity to share a way of solving that problem, when he began to date. I said, "Dickie, when you take a girl out to eat on a date, how will she know how much you want her to spend?" When he indicated he wasn't sure how to communicate this information so she wouldn't be embarrassed, I suggested that he could mention two or three choices that he thought looked good from the price range he could handle. This was just a little thing, well before Dickie needed the information, but if he hasn't used the information several times by now, I am sure he will before long.

If flowers are appropriate for the date, or there are other special hints that can be helpful, we should offer them to sons who are interested. If not, of course, we should leave them to their own devices and let them learn through their own experience.

Daughters need help, just as their male counterparts. On their first date, they may not know how to politely excuse themselves for freshening up. A simple, "Excuse me; I'll be right back" will prevent a long evening! We can suggest that a nice way to end a date is to invite their companion into the house for a few minutes. Parents can greet them and leave them to themselves for a while. This has many advantages over extended parking in the driveway! Sharing a bit of dessert and conversation in the home promotes the kind of relationship both we and our children want.

What about specific guidelines for our offsprings' dating? Do we let them adopt their own and hope for the best, or do we exercise direct supervision. Ideally, we will have established a good degree of family unity and practiced preparatory training, before our children even reached the teenage years. We will have shown that we approve of fun and excitement, as well as study and work. We will have helped them build friendships with children we believe will have a positive influence by the schools we select, the church we attend, the friends we choose, the neighborhood we live in, and the guidance, training, and example we have been offering for years. We will have carried out a natural process of wholesome sex education so our children are well aware of their bodies' functions and developing a beginning understanding of the meaning of love and the role of sexual intercourse. And we will have shown the way to a personal relationship with Christ and a solid commitment to biblical morality. If we have taken these steps together, entrance into teen dating will not introduce large, new hurdles in the form of dating principles. But we have been talking about the "ideal," which rarely fits a family perfectly.

No matter how great the relationship with our teenagers has been, we will likely have to initiate a few principles and even limits that have not been needed previously. Here I want to emphasize that I am offering suggestions—not rules—you may use in guiding your adolescents through early dating years. Teenagers need guidelines—or carefully thought-out limits—during this time, but no two teenagers mature at the same rate and no two family situations are exactly the same. The suggested principles offered here are not for blanket application, but are intended to stimulate your thinking and action. All of these guidelines have an exception at some time or place. My hope is that as you look toward your adolescents' dating, and as you help them make some choices, these guidelines will be grist for the mill.

Interest in dating generally begins during the junior-high-school years—especially for girls. Boys' interests sharpen a little later. I see no good reason for formal, unsupervised dating by seventh and eighth-grade children. If your son or daughter becomes interested in someone of the opposite sex at this age, let them see each other at school or pal around informally. A natural friendship is healthy—assuming you know and approve of the friend. But at this age, the early adolescent is just not ready for serious dating. Junior highers are often pushed into a social world of dating, sophisticated dress, and older-peer influence which they simply are not ready to handle. Hence the need for specific guidelines and supervision.

If our young teens are not happy with the limits we set, we should talk over the matter with them and listen carefully to their wishes and opinions. But we must remember that we have some experiences and wisdom they do not, and we should let them know that we just feel this is a little too early to begin formal dating. We can also let them know *when* we will allow this, so he or she will have something to anticipate.

Until dating begins, it is important to encourage our teenagers socially. Special efforts to entertain teen friends at our home will ease young people toward adult relationships. Volunteering to sponsor church outings for teens will promote healthy friendships. Supervised group activities are excellent ways of broadening young teens' social experiences. And that makes excellent preparation for later formal dating.

When our teenagers reach their freshman and sophomore years of high school (fourteen and fifteen), they are ready to assume some responsibility in dating experience. This doesn't mean that they are ready for regular dating nor that they are abnormal if dating doesn't attract them. But their level of maturity does warrant their trying their wings, if they wish to participate. They will concurrently be extending the informal boy-girl relationships and occasionally having a "real date" at some group event. I would not allow a thirteen- or fourteen-year-old girl, however, to date a seventeen- or eighteen-year-old boy. Even though girls mature more rapidly than boys, the typical freshman girl is not ready to handle the potential intimacies and the responsibilities of dating a boy that much older. I would also not allow a son or daughter this age to go to an unchaperoned party, and I would be hesitant about unchaperoned beach dates. The same goes for any type of trip when another teenager is driving a group of friends. This activity has a big appeal for thirteen- and fourteen-year-olds, but the hazards of reckless driving, negative peer influence, and of "just cruising" make this generally inadvisable at this age.

By the time teenagers reach their last two years of high school (ages sixteen to eighteen), they need a great deal more freedom in their dating and social activities in general. At this age, they are mature enough to "single date," to regularly use the family car and, if they feel strongly about it, to date one person steadily. By then parents have had fifteen years to instill positive moral and spiritual values in their children. They have helped develop social skills. And the older teens have the intellectual capacity to see the consequences of their choices and to plan more wisely. Though some parents decide to prohibit their adolescents from "going steady," and some still exert a lot of control, it seems more profitable to influence actions through discussion rather than through arbitrary limits or commands.

During this period, teenagers still need a reasonable curfew, and parents have both the right and responsibility to know where their offspring are and whom they are with. But frankly, we cannot control everything they do on their dates. If they "fall in love" at seventeen, we may reason and discuss the situation with them. We may suggest they wait a year or two before they marry. And we may suggest they take a job first and allow themselves a little time. But if they have their minds set on being married as soon as they graduate, there is little we can do. To threaten to boycott the wedding or give an ultimatum will only make things worse. I have *never* seen a positive result from this kind of situation!

If our teens become involved sexually with their steady, we may as well recognize we cannot stop it by our controls. We can counsel, advise, and suggest. And we may even forbid them to see each other. But if they really want to see each other, they will find a way. They will meet at school, or on the sly. Although we may relieve our feelings of guilt or responsibility by forbidding them to see each other, this really doesn't help. In fact, it may push them toward greater deceit and stir up unnecessary resentment toward us. It is much better to have a heart-to-heart talk and gently confront them with our concerns. We will continually pray for them. And we should be working to maintain a positive relationship. But beyond that there are real limits as to what we can do.

By the time our teenagers turn eighteen, we have to leave their dating almost entirely in their hands. We can still register approval or disapproval, but they must have freedom to shape their dating life as they desire. Hopefully, we will have a sufficiently positive relationship that they will discuss their dating and their expectations for a mate. And we are favored, indeed, if they will seek out our advice, or use us as a sounding board. Many young people continue this well into their twenties. But parental control has passed to teen control. We can serve as a mature parent-friend who offers emotional support and wise counsel. But we can no longer parent in terms of setting rules or limits on their dating.

17

Sex in Adolescence

A national survey of adolescents between thirteen and nineteen years of age found that 52 percent had engaged in premarital intercourse at least once, as reported by Robert Sorensen in *Adolescent Sexuality in Contemporary America.* As the age increased, of course, the percentage became much higher. This statistic is frightening to many parents, and it should cause us serious concern. Many adolescents are in headlong gallop toward sexual experimentation that can leave them with deep hurts and serious scars.

There is a positive side to these figures, however. Note that 48 percent of this sample had not engaged in premarital intercourse! And the same researcher found that the majority of virgins were at least fairly regular church attenders, while only a third of the nonvirgins reported any kind of regular church attendance. These figures should give Christian parents encouragement. Sometimes we wonder if our spiritual training really makes a difference in nitty-gritty areas like this. Obviously it does!

Before leaving the topic of dating and sex, let's take a few minutes to think about the process of sexual education and guidance during adolescence. Ideally we will have come a long way in the process of helping our teenagers develop positive attitudes about their sexuality by the time they reach the beginning of adolescence. Our teenagers will have a positive attitude toward their masculinity or femininity, because of positive relationships with us. They will see sex as a normal part of life and feel comfortable using appropriate words for bodily parts and sexual activities. They will not feel guilty or ashamed about the topic of sex. They will know we are comfortable with the topic. They will know how babies are conceived, how they develop within their mother, and how they are born. And they will understand that sexual intercourse and childbearing are designed by God as a vital part of marriage.

If you think your teenagers or preteenagers have not moved a good way in this direction, you might benefit greatly by reading a good book or two on sex education. One that I have found helpful is *From Parent to Child about Sex* by Wilson Grant (Zondervan). Reading and discussing a book like this can help us with our own anxieties, as well as give some good possibilities for sharing naturally with our teenagers in this vital area of life.

No matter how successful we have been in our early years, however, adolescence does bring a few new challenges. Openness is probably the single most important ingredient of effective sexual education during adolescence, as well as in the earlier years. To the degree that we are comfortable talking about our bodies and sexual processes, our offspring will tend to adopt good attitudes toward their sexuality. And to the degree we are uncomfortable, embarrassed, or ashamed of our bodies and our sexuality, our teenagers are likely to develop similar attitudes.

From the earliest years of life, children need to recognize their bodies and their sexual functions are God-given and good. We should name bodily parts and functions by using terms like *penis, breast, vagina,* and *intercourse,* when appropriate. They are not forbidden or shameful words, though they are to be used discreetly. If we get embarrassed and hesitate to call a bodily part or process by its proper term, our children sense our own anxiety and begin to think that sex is somehow "bad," frightening, or something to keep quiet about. This, of course, increases children's curiosity and spurs them to seek more information from friends, books, magazines, and movies. These sources surround sexuality with an aura of secretiveness, or sensationalism, distorting the facts and producing negative emotions of fear and guilt.

During adolescence, the openness begun in childhood should continue. By this time, of course, discussion of topics are different, because our teenagers are already quite knowledgeable about some areas of sexuality. Discussions about contraceptives, petting, premarital sex and pregnancy can all be extremely helpful to our teenagers, if they occur in the normal course of conversation and are handled without undo anxiety.

Take the matter of "the pill" as an example. Some parents have real struggles over the advisability of talking about this issue with their teens. On the one hand, they would like to be sure that their teenage daughters do not get pregnant out of wedlock. On the other, they don't want to give them any ideas by bringing up the topic! Let me encourage you to feel free to discuss premarital contraception with them. The chances are your teens are already aware of the issues. If not, it is high time they learn. But *be careful*. Don't get real serious, sit them down and let them know you "want to have a talk"! Instead, look for natural opportunities to discuss the subject of pregnancy: the world's population, the size of your own family, or a local girl who has gotten pregnant out of wedlock.

All of these can give us a natural opportunity to make sure our teenagers know about contraceptives. Frankly, if we have been open about our own and our children's sexuality, they are probably well aware of at least the basics of contraception by the time they reach adolescence. If you have used any form of contraception, it is likely your kids have raised questions which you have answered with a forthright response, such as, "That's a pill

Mother takes so her body won't produce eggs or ovum, because we have decided we already have just the right-size family."

Open talk about contraceptives with our teenagers has several advantages. The first is that it tells them contraception is no big deal. They don't have to sneak around to gain their information about sex. We can talk about it with them freely. Nearly all adults use contraceptives of one kind or another. We do because we do not want a larger family. We assume they will not need them before marriage because of their Christian standards, but they may as well know that some of their friends are probably using them and that others may wish they had!

The inclusion of sex-education programs in public and private schools is an area of concern for many parents. Ideally, sexual education should be carried out in the home and in the church. Realistically, however, the majority of parents are not adequately preparing their children to face the challenges of adult sexuality. Therefore, it is understandable that schoolteachers and administrators are stepping in to fill the gap.

Unfortunately, this puts Christian parents in a bind. We know all teenagers need constructive sex education, but we also know that effective sex education cannot be taught apart from a set of moral and spiritual values. Probably the best solution is for us to get involved at the local-school level to see that the sex-education program being given is carried out by responsible, mature individuals with a respect for moral and spiritual values.

In addition to this, we must be willing to fulfill our own responsibility to our offspring, so that any negative influences communicated at school will not adversely affect our adolescents. They should have already been well taught about both the anatomical facts of sexuality, and the moral, spiritual, and emotional foundations of mature sexuality. Our own open and effective sex education will be more than enough to counteract any negative influences from less-than-ideal training at school.

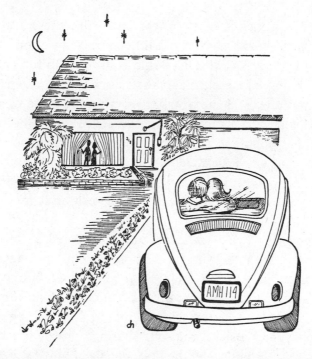

Open discussion also eliminates some of the appeal of gutter language, sexual stories, and exploitive accounts that many teenagers engage in. In other words, our frankness is good prevention. A final obvious value is that in case our teenagers do become overly involved sexually, they will not have to suffer the additional problem of a pregnancy. I personally see no need to warn our teenagers to be sure to use contraceptives, if they decide to have intercourse. I assume that, if we have a good relationship with our teens and that if they are committed spiritually, they will be able to control themselves. To warn or threaten them about pregnancy is really saying, "I don't trust you." And this is one of the best ways to push a teenager toward premarital sexual experiences! If they know about contraceptives, they are old enough to make their own decisions, in case they do become involved in premarital sexual encounters.

The same principle of openness and naturalness applies to petting. Most of us had at least a little experience of our own in this area, and our knowledge should contribute to the guidance given without making our mistakes or practices a blueprint for our children's eyes. Some of us are afraid to hint we were ever tempted by attractions of the opposite sex. We just keep quiet about it and hope and pray our children will somehow reach their wedding day unscathed. Others are tempted to use their own experiences to frighten their teenagers away from close encounters of the sexual kind. A balanced position is much more helpful.

Our teenagers will be relieved and encouraged to know that we struggled with some of the same problems they face. Our frankness can help them form definite guidelines about conduct on a date, instead of ignoring the problem. They will respect us for being open and honest with them and they will be able to gain support and insight from our sharing. On the other hand, they don't want to know all the gory details of how far you went with everybody you dated before you met your spouse! They can hear those stories from their peers. What they want from you is an understanding parent, who is aware of some of the struggles they are facing, and who has made enough progress in resolving them that they can be supportive listeners and, when asked, can offer helpful suggestions.

If your teenager goes too far in physical involvement, your most critical time of parental influence has arrived. In such a moment we are tempted to respond with anger, fear, or confusion. What is needed is self-control first, then careful listening to your son or daughter, and only then our deliberate and prayerful counsel.

After you get a grip on your emotions, draw your adolescent out. Let him tell you what has happened and how he sees the situation now. This helps the young person to think through the problem and begin thoughtful reaction. The actual condition must be confirmed, the options available carefully explored, and adjustments planned for relationships with people and with God.

Pregnancy out of wedlock is very serious, no matter what consequential steps are taken. But parents' compassionate assistance may prevent the ruin or blighting of a whole life. Parental forgiveness will help teens understand that God is a forgiving and loving Father.

Our role in family-sex education grows through the years. Either wisdom or grievous experience will eventually convince us of its great importance. Next to spiritual training, healthy development of sexuality is one of our most far-reaching influences.

As parents of teenagers, we realize our teens have to make some of their own decisions and live with the results. If those decisions fall short of our standard, our teenagers need a listening ear and sympathetic understanding, not stinging criticism and rejection. If we are able to lovingly help them through a crisis or a failure, they will learn to avoid another one, and perhaps draw closer to the One who provides strength and wisdom for successful decisions.

18

Disciplining Adolescents

By the time our offspring reach the teenage years, most of us have some well-established methods of discipline and correction. If we have developed a leadership style that is relatively cool, calm, and consistent, we can continue that approach with good results. But if we have followed a pattern of nagging, pressuring, and coercing, we may be in for trouble. Authoritarian methods of discipline that emphasize power and control may have gotten us through the first decade of parenting without obvious problems. When it comes to adolescents, however, these attitudes and techniques precipitate conflict. Not only does authoritarian direction fail to control teen conduct, it makes enemies instead of friends.

By the time our offspring are in their teenage years, they know instinctively they deserve to be treated with respect. They believe they should have a part in family planning. And they expect to have some straightforward discussions with us. To discipline effectively during adolescence, we must treat our teenagers as the near-adults they are. Although this is not primarily a book on discipline, the subject is vital for our parent-teen relationship. In *Help! I'm a Parent* (Zondervan) I deal in much greater depth with the topic of discipline.

A good beginning point is to realize that *teenagers still need pa-*

rental guidance and direction. Sometimes we think teenagers want no part of parental advice, correction, or supervision. This is not the case for most teenagers. They know they are not adults and they recognize their need for loving limits and sensitive supervision. We need not apologize for setting limits or correcting, and we should not expect negative reactions to good discipline and training. Strong resistance arises when we fail to realize our teenagers are more mature than they used to be, and that our old methods are not necessarily appropriate for adolescents.

A second guiding principle is that *power will no longer work.* When children are young we can spank them, carry them to their rooms, banish them from our presence, or force them to stay inside as discipline. By the time our children reach teenage years, these methods are either impossible, undesirable or both. I know one father that takes pride in the fact that he stood in the doorway and barred his eighteen-year-old from leaving the house. He indeed kept his son home. But resorting to such brute force is a sure sign we have lost control of our teenagers and don't know how to handle them more wisely. This also means that spankings are out for adolescents. I firmly believe there is a place for spankings. (*See* Proverbs 22:15.) But we should never spank a child in anger and we should never attempt to correct a teenager by spanking. Although we might appear to get away with it, it does no lasting good and only creates fear or resentment in our adolescents.

There are many more effective means of disciplining a teenager. Slapping, spanking, or in any way using physical force on a teenager communicates a lack of respect, and only tells them we are at our wit's end and don't know what to do! Sometimes we think this will show the teenager who is boss. But the moment we decide to show anyone who is boss we have just let them know that *they* are! The mature parent, who is sensitive to his teenagers and aware of some constructive means of discipline, can lovingly exercise his authority. He doesn't have to fight to win it!

One concept that has been helpful to many parents is the fact that discipline is not the same as punishment. Most of us use the terms interchangeably. But a closer look shows that they are different concepts, and that we can fall into some very counterproductive patterns if we fail to understand the differences.

According to the Bible, punishment is penalty inflicted for sin. Punishment is designed to bring justice or revenge against wrongdoers. Isaiah, for example, records God's warning: "I will punish the world for their evil, and the wicked for their iniquity; and I will cause the arrogancy of the proud to cease, and will lay low the haughtiness of the terrible (13:11 KJV).

In contrast, the purpose of discipline is to promote growth. The author of Hebrews tell us: "Our fathers disciplined us for a little while as they thought best; but God disciplines us for our good, that we may share in his holiness" (12:10). When Christ was crucified for our sins, He once and for all paid the penalty for all of the sins of His children. Since the penalty for our sins is paid, He responds to us in constructive discipline. He corrects us, in other words, to help us grow—*not* to make us suffer for our wrongdoing.

The focus of punishment and discipline is also very different. Since punishment is designed to even the score for misbehaviors, it focuses on past misdeeds. Discipline, in contrast, focuses on future positive attitudes and actions.

The attitude of the person exercising the correction is also different in discipline and punishment. In punishment, the attitude is anger. In discipline, the attitude is love. Revelation 3:19 tells us, "Those whom I love I rebuke and discipline. . . ." God's discipline may involve pain—just as ours may—as a necessary corrective influence. But the objective is positive and our attitude is loving rather than punitive.

Just as God never punishes His children, we should never punish ours. Romans 12:19 tells us " 'It is mine to avenge; I will repay,' says the Lord." We should discipline or correct them— but we should never punish. The essential difference is this: If we become angry at our teenagers and speak harshly, ground them, or forbid them some other privilege, we are probably doing it to get even. They have disobeyed us, or violated our standards, and we are not going to put up with it. This kind of angry reaction, however, either breeds a neurotic type of conformity, or leads to increased anger and rebellion. Our teenagers sense we are responding out of our own anger and desires to "even the score," rather than out of a real love and concern for their welfare. On the other hand, if we sit down quietly with our teenagers and discuss the matter, try to understand their viewpoint, and then decide an appropriate way of improving the situation, they will sense our love and concern and will be much more likely to respond favorably. Punishment is essentially a ventilation of our own anger, while discipline is a thoughtful and loving way of training our adolescents.

I realize that most of us will occasionally become angry with our teenagers. It is impossible to live in intimate contact with others and not experience some misunderstandings and hard feelings. But when we sense these feelings coming, we should postpone discipline. We should let our spouse handle the situation or defer intervention, until we have cooled off. We may need to tell our teenager, "I am too angry now to talk rationally about this. After I have settled down, we will talk." This allows us to regain the composure and balance that aid effective communication and good discipline. It also enables us to avoid blaming our teenagers for our emotional responses.

When we become angry with someone, most of us tend to say something, such as, "You make me so angry!" But if we stop and think about it, this is not really a true picture of the situation.

When we say, "You make me so angry!" we are putting the responsibility for our feelings onto our teenagers. We are blaming them for our emotional responses. A more accurate way of expressing our feelings is to say, "I feel very upset when you do that!" This statement puts the responsibilities where they really belong. Our teenagers cannot really make us angry. They can only do things to which we respond with anger. Teens have a responsibility for their actions, but we have a responsibility for our *r*eactions. This clarification of responsibilities tends to make us both less defensive (and offensive!) and encourages more effective communication and discipline. This chart adapted from *A Guide to Child Rearing* summarizes the main differences between *discipline* and *punishment*.

	Punishment	Discipline
Purpose	Justice, or to inflict penalty for an offense	Promote maturity and growth
Focus	Past misdeeds	Future correct attitudes and actions
Attitude of Parent Figure	Anger	Love
Resulting Behavior	Conformity or rebellion	Growth
Resulting Emotion	Fear, guilt, or anger	Love and security

Another important thought to keep in mind is that *discipline is more than correction.* Sometimes we fall into the habit of assuming discipline is simply what we do *after* our children get into some type of misbehavior. But this is not the case. When Christ "disciplined" His twelve helpers, He didn't hover about waiting for mistakes that He could correct. He spent three years of His life pouring Himself into His disciples. He lived with them, ate with them, slept with them, and taught them. He instructed them and trained them. And He used lessons from life to communicate important truths. Although He did correct them and discipline them in the narrow sense of the word, reacting to their mistakes was only a small part of His whole process of training and discipline. This should be true for our relations with our adolescents also.

They need our good example. They need a listening ear. They need our suggestions—sometimes! And they need our encouragement and support. If we limit our interactions to times when they are in trouble, it will probably be too late! We have to earn their respect and the right to be heard in order to make our advice serviceable. In fact, as the teenage years progress, we should find ourselves giving less corrections or instructions. Instead, we should be talking things over, getting their opinions, and helping them make their own choices.

Another ingredient of effective discipline is learning to *carry one's share of family responsibilities*. Every teenager should be responsible for cleaning up his own room, taking care of his own things, and handling one or more chores around the house. The jobs can be almost anything. Typically, they involve taking out the trash, washing dishes, washing the car, mowing the yard, shoveling snow, or dusting and vacuuming periodically. It should be relatively easy to divvy up the family chores. When someone doesn't carry out his responsibility, we should utilize a "logical consequence" to help him learn more dependability.

Logical consequences are probably the best ways of helping children learn to carry out their task around the home. The concept of logical consequences was popularized in our age by Dr. Rudolph Dreikurs. Long before Dreikurs, however, the Bible gave several examples of natural and logical consequences. They are also a good way of handling a variety of other problems. Simply put, a logical consequence is some event or consequence that is agreed upon beforehand by the parent and teen which will come to pass if one's responsibilities are not fulfilled. For example, if your son is in charge of feeding the family pet and his job is not done by the time evening rolls around, it is logical that he does not have a meal either!

There is no need to nag, coerce, or remind. When chores are assigned, we should decide with our offspring what the consequences will be if they "forget" to do their jobs. Then we can write down this little agreement and forget about it, until their first "omission." At that time we say, "Sorry, John. If Bowser doesn't eat, neither do you!" The same principle applies to un-

washed cars or uncut lawns. If the car is not washed by the appointed day, it is logical that your son will not be able to use the car that week. And if the yard remains unmowed, it is logical that your son not practice basketball or head to the beach, until it is done. We don't need to resort to angry threats or condemnations. We simply agree ahead of time and carry out the consequence.

When it comes to curfew violations, the same principle of consequences will work wonders. The logical consequence for staying out past curfew is to be grounded for a reasonable period. This period should be mutually decided upon ahead of time, so that we all agree that it is fair and then calmly carried out. But there are logical exceptions! Maybe they really did run out of gas! Or maybe something very important did come up, and it was impossible to notify you. If this is the case, don't hold rigidly to a rule. Be ready to make an exception, but be sure there is good reason for it. Don't let incipient slyness con you out of your responsibility to teach your teenagers to be responsible!

The use of logical consequences leads me to my last suggestion. With teenagers *it is vitally important that we formulate together the possible consequences of failing to carry out one's responsibilities ahead of time.* We should not conduct this in a threatening manner, nor suggest that we expect they *will* violate curfew, forget their chores, or get into some kind of trouble. We can say something, such as, "Since your responsibility is to wash the car by Saturday morning, what could we do to help you remember, since we all get busy and tend to forget?" If you use this approach, your teenager will get the message and probably suggest that if he fails to wash the car, he can't use it that week, or some other appropriate consequence. Then you can agree and go on about your business. This way there are no surprises, and you won't be tempted to come up with some punitive action if he fails to wash the car. This type of arrangement, by the way, is not punitive at all. It is a calm, sensitive form of constructive discipline. Punishment is something we do in anger of frustration in an attempt to pay our children back for misbehaviors. Discipline is a positive and constructive approach to training.

Before leaving our topic of discipline, I have just one more suggestion. We need to remember that our efforts at discipline will be no more successful than the quality of our overall relationship with our teenagers. Everything we have said in the previous chapters is related to discipline. If we understand our teenagers' needs, if we are sensitive to their feelings, and if we have open and ongoing communication, discipline will not be a serious problem during the adolescent years. But if our teenagers feel misunderstood, left out, or resentful, no amount of correction will really solve the problem. Effective discipline can only grow from the soil of mutual acceptance and respect.

19

Alcohol and Drugs

"The times they are a-changing," chant the pop singers, and observers of the teen world have to agree. The new problem is pervasive—illegal drugs among teenagers. Coupled with the age-old use of alcohol this presents a difficult problem and one without any pat or simple answers.

We have to face the fact that a large majority of teenagers experiment with some form of drug or alcohol, despite their parents' disapproval. Whether it is marijuana, speed, reds, blues, uppers, downers, or LSD, most teenagers experiment with one or more of the currently popular drugs. In addition, every secular high-school campus (and some Christian ones) have a very significant number of regular users and several—if not many—drug pushers. A television special recently reported that nearly one-third of all teenagers consider themselves regular users of some type of drug! And one-third of all teenagers in America get drunk at least once a month!

Our family happens to live in a relatively conservative area—at least for California! There is a strong Christian influence in our town. We are very near a rural area, and we don't have the problems of a ghetto school. Yet drugs are easily accessible on our high-school campus and are a common part of many teenage parties and get-togethers.

Not far from our home is a new shopping mall. It has a Broadway, a Sears, a Robinson's, a Penney's, and nearly a hundred other shops and stores. It also has several nice restaurants and some family entertainments. On most evenings or weekends, I am told, you can find one or more teenage drugs pushers there!

Drugs have moved steadily from college circles to high-school campuses and increasingly are found in junior-high schools. Occasionally we hear of drug use as early as the fourth or fifth grades of elementary schools! With such easy access and such widespread usage, it does no good to stick our heads in the sand and assume that drugs are really a minor problem, or one that probably will not confront our teens. No matter how decent your son or daughter is, he or she will have ample opportunity to be tempted to experiment with drugs, or to use them regularly if desired. And you might have to face the shock of a phone call from the police about your daughter's drunkenness, or of finding your son spaced out on drugs.

I am writing this particularly for Christian parents, so I am not dealing with the drug scene that faces families who have no strong scruples against it. In many segments of our society, drugs have become accepted among adults as well as teens. Some parents rely heavily on alcohol or other drugs. They regularly get high or loaded and assume their teenagers will occasionally do the same. They just hope their kids will use a little common sense and not get in too much trouble. In other sections of our culture, a gang or clique will have its own drug life-style. No one is really "in," unless he fully participates. You and I need to know that this exists and that our teenagers are surrounded by this influence, but if we have strong moral and spiritual commitments, and if we have done a reasonably good job of rearing our children to the point of adolescence, the chances are greatly reduced that we will have serious problems in this area.

Our problems are more likely to involve experimenting with drugs, our consequent attitudes, and relationships with our children's friends that use drugs periodically. Here are a few guidelines and suggestions, if you and your teens fall in this general category.

To begin with, *you do not need to assume that every teenager—including yours—is going to experiment with drugs.* Although the percentage of teens who never use drugs is dismayingly small, there are large numbers of young people who pass through their teenager years without ever trying drugs at all. And many of these don't even bother to have a drink of alcohol. I say this because some people would have us think that taking drugs is a complete inevitability. They assume that every adolescent is going to do it and that those few who don't, probably resist because of some neurotic inhibitions, rather than any degree of personal maturity.

This is just not true. If you have a very good relationship with your teenager, and if he shares your moral and spiritual values, there is a very good possibility that he will bypass drugs entirely. We should not assume there is no possibility of this happy situation!

A good way to prepare your adolescents to resist drugs is to *talk calmly about the subject whenever it arises.* Many parents tend to go to one of two extremes. We either ignore the problem and hope it will go away, or we rant uncontrollably and are extremely dogmatic and outspoken. We threaten our preteenagers and early teens with horror stories about drugs, and let them know they are expected to keep a million miles away. We tell them a little grass is likely to lead to other drugs, and if they are not careful, they will end up heroin addicts. These scare tactics take the same form that the threat did when we were growing up: that if we had one drink, we might become alcoholics. Although it is true that there has never been an alcoholic who didn't take a first drink, it is also true that there are many people who do have an occasional social drink and never suffer from it!

We need to be very careful not to twist and distort the truth when we are discussing something as significant as potential drug abuse. We may feed our children a pack of lies and exaggerations about the harmful effects of alcohol or drugs when they are younger, but when they reach their adolescent years, they are going to find out differently. They will meet some of the top athletes and popular kids at school who smoke a little grass and seem none the worse for wear. When they begin to find this out, they can only come to one conclusion: Either we were lying to them or we just didn't know what we were talking about! And once we lose our credibility, it is extremely difficult to have any further positive influence.

A much more successful approach is to be completely honest and open with our teens. When asked about drugs or alcohol, try to answer the questions accurately and calmly. Let them know that the Bible teaches self-control in every area, and that it specifically forbids excessive use of alcohol. Let them know that drugs like heroin are extremely dangerous and can literally destroy one's life. And let them know that everything in between can lead to serious problems. We should calmly share with them why we believe we should avoid all drug usage, but we shouldn't try to convince them that everyone who pops a pill is on the road to a lifetime of addiction. If we maturely point out the liabilities of drug use and let them know why we choose to abstain, they are very likely to follow our example. They may decide to experiment once or twice, but that will satisfy their curiosity.

At this point I would like to clarify one potential misunderstanding. In stressing the need to quietly and considerately discuss the problem of alcohol and drug abuse with our adolescents, I am not suggesting we take a weak, passive, or wish-washy approach to the problem. I personally think drugs are one of the greatest menaces to our society, and I have seen firsthand the results of alcohol abuse. I wish neither of these existed. But since they do, we have to face reality. To either ignore the potential problem in a permissive way, or to think we can force our offspring to avoid all temptation in the areas by authoritarian scare tactics is only sticking our heads in the sand. The only workable solution is to be open and honest about the issue, knowing that our teens will someday have to decide for themselves. The best way we can prepare them for that time is to calmly and without exaggeration discuss both their understanding of the drug scene and our own moral convictions. If we have a relationship of mutual respect and trust, this should be sufficient deterrent to this potentially serious problem.

If you discover your teenager is experimenting with drugs, *your best ally is self-control.* I realize the natural reaction is anger and panic. But when this happens, we tend to either condemn our teenagers, or in some way vent our anger and put them down. This only accentuates the problem. Although it may be hard, try to sit quietly and draw your adolescent out. Ask him about his experience. Find out how it came about. And let him share just how it felt. Chances are he will be well aware that it was scary, unnecessary, harmful, or at best a temporary high that served as an escape or was tried to put off a little peer-group pressure. If you can listen calmly, it will go a long way in helping him come to you with other problems and in building up his sense of trust and confidence in you.

Closely related to the ability to talk candidly and realistically about drugs with our teenagers is our willingness *to take time to get some facts.* If you don't know more about drugs than your teenager, he will not listen to you long on the subject. Take time to read up on the subject, to attend a seminar, or to seek out some information from local police officials or agencies. This will increase your understanding and make your counsel more credible—assuming you don't start holding yourself out as an expert and preaching about the evils of drugs! Be sure to use your information cautiously, and don't be afraid to learn from your teenagers too. The chances are they may already know more than you!

Another important principle for understanding teenage drug abuse is: *Teenagers who seriously abuse drugs generally do so for one of two reasons. They either travel in a subculture where this is accepted practice, or else they have significant emotional disturbances or family conflicts.* Assuming that the former is not true in your son's or daughter's case, let's take a look at the role of emotional disturbance. Why would a teenager from a relatively normal Christian home become involved in drugs? The answer is usually that he is an unhappy person. Perhaps he is depressed and seeking a synthetic escape. Perhaps he is resentful toward you or your spouse, and sees this as a way of hurting you or proclaiming his independence. Perhaps he is overwhelmed by personal inadequacy or failure in the responsibilities of adolescence, or perhaps a personality disorder weakens his ability to act responsibly. These may activate a teenager to go beyond the experimental stage.

When this happens, it is too late to read another book! I strongly recommend you seek a professional counselor or psychotherapist who can relate to both you and your teenager. To correct this condition, you are going to have to invest some time and money to determine the deep cause or causes of the problem and begin to make some significant changes. As long as our teenagers are depressed, confused, or unhappy at home, we have no basis to help them move away from drugs. Although drugs compound personal problems, the habituated individual sees no reason to give up the relief they afford, unless the destructive elements are removed from his life.

In a similar way, as long as our teenagers harbor strong feelings of resentment toward us, any effort to get them to give up their drugs will only push them to rebel, reinforce their usage, and make continued abuse more likely!

20

Disinterest in Church

I rarely go through a meeting with parents without being asked, "Should we force our teenagers to go to church?" This is a much more complicated question than it first seems. We desire to train our children spiritually, so we naturally want to expose them to Christian friends, worship, and biblical instruction. But during the teenage years, we often find our offspring losing interest in church gatherings, or even becoming antagonistic.

As I have stressed throughout, a good way to understand our teenagers is to put ourselves in their shoes. This is especially important in understanding their feelings about church. Start with a little honest introspection. Don't you occasionally get bored in church services? Don't you sometimes find your mind wandering and yourself losing interest in what is going on? And don't you sometimes do little more than fill a space in the pew?

It may be that the preacher just doesn't "turn us on." What he says may be all right but not presented in an especially interesting way; or maybe there is rarely anything really new or challenging. Sometimes we hear the same thing so often, it becomes old hat. If this happens to us, it is certainly understandable for adolescents. Oriented to excitement, challenge, and interesting activities, nothing seems duller to active teens than listening to a boring sermon! *A starting place, therefore, for understanding our teen-*

agers' attitudes toward church is to ask ourselves if there is really much there that would interest the average healthy or typical adolescent.

This means not only the sermon, but also the Sunday-school class, the youth leaders, and the other teenagers that participate. Many teenagers complain that their church youth group is "duddy." Sometimes the student leaders are cliquish, arrogant, or in some way "out of it." Because peer acceptance is so important to the teenager, your adolescent may not want to be associated with these people. This isn't his idea of fellowship! It's not that he doesn't like them. It's just that they don't really hold his interest or fulfill his social needs.

Such problems may be complicated by a rigid and legalistic approach to the Christian life. Such church leaders place more emphasis on what Christians should avoid rather than on what they enjoy. They propagate a list of *don'ts* that have been variously labeled "the sinful seven," "the evil eight," or "the dirty dozen." These church leaders warn them not to drink, or smoke, or dance. They warn teens about the evils of movies or other forms of entertainment. And they constantly harp on certain forms of dress or music they believe are especially evil or inappropriate. Although some teenagers manage to accept these standards uncritically, many others do not. At this point, I am not saying whether the particular activities are right or wrong. I am simply stating that some teenagers are repelled by an array of religious *dos* and *don'ts*.

This focus on prohibitions is often related to a general approach to the Christian life that emphasizes external actions and an excess of guilt motivation and pressure. Rather than focusing on God's provisions of love, guidance, and strength, teenagers are repeatedly told what they must not do. The scale highlights conformity and performance, rather than our response to all that Christ has done for us.

In other cases, teenagers turn against church as an expression of anger toward their parents. When church life is important to parents, teens know they can irritate or upset us by spurning the thing that is closest to us. In this instance, the church is not the teens' real target.

When our teenagers lose interest in church because of uninteresting teaching, or because there are few other young people that attract them, we have a couple of options. *Perhaps we can get involved with the youth program directly or indirectly and help build it up.* Teenagers can put up with numerous deficiencies if they find the friendships and social fulfillment they need at church. If, however, there seems no way to improve the teen ministry substantially, you should seriously consider changing churches.

Now I realize you may have been in your church for twenty

years or more, and that the pastor is a personal friend. Your social life may revolve around the church, or you may be so involved, you don't even want to *consider* the possibility! You're first reaction is "No way. This is *our* church and our teenagers had better learn to adapt to it!" This is an entirely normal reaction, but let me ask you to stay with me for a moment and reconsider. Our teenagers are people, too, with rights, desires, and interests like our own. If we were bored with the church or not attracted to the people in it, we would want to move. And if we would consider moving for our own sakes, isn't it reasonable to consider moving for our children's? In fact, since the teenage years are such formative ones, it may be even more important.

This doesn't mean you have to give up all your friends, nor are you necessarily making a permanent change. But if you are committed to seeing your teenagers grow spiritually and they are not happy in their present church, you should prayerfully consider a better situation. A group of sharp Christian young people and a good youth program may make an even greater impact on your teenager than all the praying and training you attempt at home.

This is not to minimize the importance of Christian training in the home. And it is surely not to underestimate the power of prayer. It is simply to acknowledge that teenagers respond very favorably to a positive peer influence and a youth program that takes both their spiritual and their social needs into consideration.

A few years ago, a Christian couple asked my suggestion about what to do for teenagers who had lost interest in their church. After a good bit of discussion, it seemed to me that there were no major problems in the family, and that the issue centered in the lack of a stimulating youth program in the church. Consequently the teenagers in this family were beginning to associate with nonchurch youth, whose negative habits and attitudes were rubbing off on the Christian young people. At my suggestion, the parents talked the matter over with their teens and asked if they would be interested in finding another church. The teenagers agreed, and they decided to visit several churches. After a few weeks, they found one the teenagers liked very much. It had a large, aggressive young people's group. Although it wouldn't have been the parents' first choice, they were satisfied they could be happy there at least through their children's adolescence.

Some time later I encountered the parents and the mother said, "You know, I think our move saved our children. They weren't bad kids, but they weren't getting what they needed from our church. Though it was a hard change for us, that is one decision we will never regret!"

Sometimes the solution is not that easy. You may live in a community where your present church is the only good option. If that is the case, you could consider encouraging your children to try a Christian youth group at school or at another church, where their partial involvement would be more rewarding.

One thought should undergird whatever planning we do about our teenager's spiritual activities. It is this: *It does absolutely no good to force older teenagers to go to a church they really cannot stand.* If we force our teenagers to go to church when they do not want to, we are likely to cause more problems than we solve. It makes them even more angry and resentful of us, and this resentment naturally carries over to God.

Frankly, forcing a teenager to go to church is often more for our sake than theirs. We believe that if we can get them into the door, the rest is up to God, the pastor, or someone else. We have fulfilled our responsibility and need no longer feel guilty for their problems! When we resort to this kind of pressure, however, our teenagers sense the limitations of our own Christianity.

Why is it, they wonder, *that my parents get angry with me and force me to go to church when I do not want to. Christianity must not be all that it's cracked up to be, if you have to force people to go!* And they are correct. Christianity is first of all an opportunity. Only later is it an obligation. God provides salvation and deliverance for us, but He doesn't force it on us. Once we see our needs and the provisions that He offers, we will naturally want to avail ourselves of them through worship, service, and fellowship. But to force teenagers to go to church gets the cart before the horse.

In stressing the inadequacy of forcing teenagers to go to a service that holds no interest for them, I am not suggesting we sit idly by and do nothing. If, after trying to improve our church's youth group, solving the family conflicts behind our teens' negativism toward spiritual things, and considering other churches or youth ministries, we *still* haven't come to a good solution, there is still another option.

Without preaching or condemning, make an agreement with a teenager who is turned off on church to attend one service each week. Instead of forcing teenagers to attend Sunday school and evening or midweek services, we can take this approach. "I realize church doesn't turn you on and I can understand that. There aren't any kids there you like and the preacher is a little boring [or loud, or whatever]. But we like to be together as a family at least one service a week. We enjoy being with you and getting dressed up and attending church together. We aren't going to force you to be there every time the doors are open, but we do want to go together for at least the morning worship service."

In taking this approach, the parents are not condemning the teenager for not liking church. They are not suggesting he is "unspiritual." And they are not telling him, "It's for your own good." All of these approaches stir up more resistance. Instead they are saying they enjoy his presence. They like to be together—and it is meaningful for them to attend church as a family.

Another approach is to let your teenagers choose one service each week—whether it is the Sunday-morning worship service, Sunday school or youth group.

At this point some parents protest, "But don't we all need to worship God and learn to listen to His Word?" Yes, of course we do. But we must remember that someone who has been dragged or shoved into a church pew will be in no mood for worship and learning. He will be sitting and stewing, just waiting to bolt that whole scene, as soon as he turns eighteen!

Before we leave this topic, I would like to offer one more observation. *Like so many other problems we encounter with our teens, bad attitudes toward church usually do not suddenly or capriciously appear during the adolescent years.* Although we may not have seen them coming, they have probably been building up for several years. Before this time, however, our children just didn't bother to express their boredom or their negative reactions. They assumed it was their duty to do as they were told, so they went through the motions. If you have preteenagers, it is important that you begin now to find out if church and Sunday school is a really meaningful experience. And if it isn't, consider doing something that will change that now. Don't wait until you hit a crisis!

If your offspring are well into their teenage years, don't think your only hope for influencing them lies in getting them to church. While this is an important experience, your relationship with your teens and the other friends they have is even more important. You can help them grow a great deal in the normal course of living if you are open, honest, and sensitive to their needs. And you can also help by seeing that they have other opportunities to interact with Christian families and teenagers. Don't try to force new friends on them, but take a little time to see if there is a family with kids your teenager's age that you would like to get to know. Go to a ball game together, or have them over for a dinner, or a swim. Sometimes good friendships begin to grow from this type of contact. These peer influences are a major determiner of your adolescents' values, morals, and commitments.

21

Money Matters

A sure sign of accelerating adolescence is the urgent need for spending money. And with this need comes a similar need to learn to manage their financial affairs. To help teenagers learn to take responsibility for their finances, most parents follow one of four arrangements.

The simplest is the *parental handout*. Under this arrangement, parents give teenagers whatever the teenager "needs"! There is no real allowance under this system, and the teenagers are not expected to work to earn any of their spending money. The parents simply assume it is their responsibility to care for their adolescents' financial needs and try as best they can to determine what these needs really are, so they will not spoil them. Some families find this system works well, but it does have a couple of potential drawbacks. To begin with, it may be difficult to determine just what is a *need* and what is a *wish*. Your teenager may think that because several boys his age have a car, he *needs* one. The truth of the matter is more likely that he *wants* one. The second problem is that a teenager who is reared under the handout method does not have as much opportunity to learn to budget his own money and begin to assume responsibilities for his finances. This lack of experience may haunt him later.

A second approach is the *you're-on-your-own method*. Under this system parents supply the basic needs of room and board and clothing. When their sons or daughters want money for special activities, snacks, gifts, or personal acquisitions, they are expected to earn it for themselves. They may find after-school jobs, or the parents supply a list of jobs for which they're willing to compensate around the home and agree to pay a set amount for them each week. This approach has the advantage of giving your teenager an opportunity to assume responsibility for his finances. It does have a couple of potential drawbacks, however. Many teenagers are too young, or do not have the opportunity to take a part-time job, handle their studies and other school activities, and maintain a decent social life. School and social activities are very important in our teenagers' development and we should try not to put them in a situation that will prematurely make

them miss out on a lot of healthy adolescent experiences. It is possible for a teenager to be "too serious" and to take on so much responsibility that he overdoes it.

Probably the most common way of handling teenage finances is *the allowance method*. This has the advantage of regular income, which gives the opportunity to learn to budget and handle money responsibly. After we've agreed on a suitable weekly or monthly allowance, it is up to the teenager to decide on the details of his budget. We can help by encouraging him to make a list of his basic expenses and optional expenses. We can also suggest a small amount be set aside for "mad money" or emergencies. If we want to teach our offspring tithing, this is also an excellent opportunity. Simply encourage them to set aside the first 10 percent of their income for the Lord's work. This could go through your local church, a missionary friend, or an organization that is especially meaningful to your offspring or your family.

I prefer the fourth—a slight adaptation of the allowance method. Rather than operating on a strict allowance, we make two alterations. The first is to encourage our children to take a part-time job, if it is available and would not interfere with other responsibilities. If something suitable isn't available during the school year, they may pick up a part-time summer job. This provides a teenager with his own money and acquaints him with the world of work. If you do this, however, I suggest that you do not simply subtract his earnings from the regular allowance. This works against incentive to produce and save. The extra income should be reward for extra effort and additional opportunities. Some teenagers decide they want a car enough to work for its purchase and maintenance. They may be able to save up enough by themselves, or they may work out an agreement with us that when they hit sixteen or seventeen, we will help them out, provided they pay for all the insurance and upkeep on the car. Other teenagers save hundreds of dollars toward their college education while they are still in high school. This guarantees an easier financial road in college and also builds personal responsibility. Some parents decide to match their children's savings from the time they are very young. This is a great incentive!

Another helpful modification of the allowance plan is to make room for special occasions or emergencies. A teenager who receives a few dollars a week just cannot be prepared to spend two hundred dollars for a special band tour to Washington, D.C., or the Rose Bowl Parade. A summer soccer camp, a formal dress, or any number of worthwhile things can come up that are beyond the reach of the tightly budgeted teenagers. When this happens we should try to help them plan ahead, so they can save what they can and earn extra money if possible. But we should also be willing to chip in and help, if needed. This approach has the advantage of giving your teenager the opportunity to learn to budget his money, to work if he can, and to cooperate with us in determining his needs and providing for them.

This method works well in issues like buying a car for your teenagers. As much as possible, this should be a shared responsibility. Your own financial situation and your teenagers' needs and ability to earn money will determine how these responsibilities are shared. If, for example, you live at a distance from high school, it may be almost essential that your teenager have his own car or ready access to the family car. Without it, he would have great difficulty participating in extracurricular activities. In this case, you may assume a much greater share of the load— perhaps even the entire amount. But if a car will be strictly a pleasure vehicle, not really necessary for most activities, you may expect your teenager to be largely responsible for its purchase and maintenance.

Some parents decide to pay for all school- and church-related activities, as well as a small allowance, and let their teenagers earn money for any other activities. All decisions on financial help for our teenagers need to balance between our God-given responsibility to provide for them and their growing need to accept responsibility for their own affairs.

I would like to give one last caution about money. Some parents withhold a son's or daughter's allowance as a means of discipline. I believe this is counterproductive. An allowance should be recognized as a parental provision to meet acknowledged needs at a certain age of development. To revoke or diminish an allowance is really a punitive act, rather than a positive corrective one, and it will only stir up resentment and rebellion. There are a hundred more effective ways of disciplining than taking away an allowance!

22

Coping With Conflict

Every home has a certain amount of conflict. No matter how well trained our family is, occasional disagreements or misunderstandings arise about important issues. They may range from where the family is going out to eat through questions of curfew and dating, to issues of taking a part-time job after school, or smoking or drinking. But whatever the issue, principles or guidelines can help us handle these situations with a minimum of hassle. In this chapter, I am limiting our discussion to specific issues where we have differences of opinions and must come to some sort of decision. I am not considering ongoing personality clashes that incite constant bickering and dissatisfaction until chapter 23.

The starting place for interpersonal problem solving is respect for the other individual. Sometimes we charge toward a dispute "loaded for bear." We know our teenagers are outrageously wrong and we are out to prove it. On the tip of our tongues are choice salvos such as, "You aren't dry behind the ears yet"; "When you grow up you will realize that we are right"; or, "You teenagers are all alike—you can't think for yourselves." Such a barrage demolishes profitable discussion. It is based on the false assumption that teenagers' ideas, wishes, and opinions are of trivial value. This attitude only creates a new problem. As soon as our teenagers sense this attitude, they respond with their own form of prejudice or character assassination. They say such things as, "You *never* listen to us." "You just don't care about anyone but yourself"; or, "You're out of touch!" Once we start this type of name calling and accusing, progress is frozen. Instead of resorting to emotional diatribes, we need to respect our teenagers and let them know it. If we really listen and try to understand their viewpoints, we set a cooperative tone for mutual discussions.

A second guideline for handling family conflicts is to *set aside a specific time to work on a problem or misunderstanding.* I realize that sometimes this is not possible. We may face a situation that requires an immediate decision. But too often we try to resolve important issues on the spot—issues that deserve varied input and calm reflection. The pressure of busy schedules urges forced communication and hurried decisions that often boomerang on us. If possible, tell your son or daughter, "This is something we need a little time to think and talk about. Let's discuss it right after the dishes are taken care of this evening." By setting a specific time, we are indicating we take our children and their concerns seriously. And both they and we will be better prepared for sound conclusions.

If you are like many parents and teenagers, your family discussions are frequently one-sided. Parents or teens monopolize the discussion, so no meaningful exchange occurs. Or if both participate, each is inclined to focus on his own words. In fact, we may just wait until the other takes a deep breath, so we can move in with our perspective! This is talking *at* instead of *with* each other.

If this is a problem in your family, a guideline for communication in highly charged topics is: *Agree beforehand that no one will voice his opinion until he has repeated to the other person's satisfaction what the first one has said.*

Let's say, for example, that you think ten-thirty is a good time for your daughter to arrive home from some evening date or school function. She prefers a later hour. The tendency is to unleash all our stored-up arguments, as if we hadn't heard what our daughter said, or down her plan without knowing the facts. A better way is to ask for information and her reasoning. She may tell us the function isn't over until ten, and then everybody goes to get a snack. There is no way she can join them and be home by ten-thirty.

After you know what is involved, you can rephrase the details to make sure you understand the situation—and she knows you understand. We might say "Let's see. If I understand you right, it seems as if the time after the party is nearly as important as the party itself. Nearly everyone stops someplace and you don't want to be left out." After our teenager has had a chance to let us know if we understood correctly, we can then share some of our perspectives or concerns.

If the outing is on a school night, we can voice that concern. If it is a weekend, we may say that our big concern is not the exact hour she comes home, but where she will be and what she will be doing until she gets home. Then your teenager can take her turn, checking her understanding of your words and feelings. She might say: "Let's see now. I think you are saying that another half hour or so wouldn't be a problem, if you knew what I was doing or where we all would be." Then she can share her reaction to this statement. From there you can move to the next step in arriving at a decision. By itself, this rule won't solve your problems, but I think you can begin to see the advantages it has. It encourages us to listen carefully and be sure we understand each other's ideas and opinions before we give our own. When we do this, we are less likely to jump too quickly or say things that stir up anger or resentment.

Another guideline is to *capitalize on areas of agreement.* Sometimes we slip into a pattern of conflict that concentrates on the aspects of disagreement. This is a subtle trap that makes things worse. All of us have a great deal in common with our teenagers, and we can nearly always find several points of agreement if we search them out. This is important because it improves the environment for making satisfying settlements.

If our teenager, for example, wants to attend a slumber party, and we tend to think she shouldn't, first look for areas of agreement. I assume that both of us want her to have fun. I assume that both want her to have friends. And I assume that we might let her spend the night at a friend's under the "right" conditions. All of these are positive areas of agreement, though they might go unrecognized if left unsaid. Then specify the areas of our differences or concern. Perhaps we don't know the other girl's parents. Perhaps it is on a weeknight. Perhaps we don't know the other girls, or perhaps we have heard there is a lot of drinking at

some slumber parties. Then take these issues one by one and try to come to a better understanding. But don't forget our areas of agreement. Use them as a base from which to work.

The apostle Paul wrote, ". . . When I am with Gentiles who follow Jewish customs and ceremonies I don't argue, even though I don't agree, because I want to help them" (1 Corinthians 9:20 The Living Bible). In contrast, many of us would have written, "When I am with my teenagers who follow local customs, I don't argue *unless* I disagree, because I want to help them!" Paul was communicating a strategic truth about how to influence others. He was suggesting that it is best to find the common ground and keep our disagreements to a minimum. When others—including our own teenagers—see that we are concerned with finding mutual understanding, they will be more open to our influence.

Another suggestion is to *look for a mutually satisfying compromise.* Maybe you can agree to let your daughter go, after learning more firsthand about the parents of the girl who is having the slumber party. Maybe you could get the time switched to a weekend instead of a weeknight. Or maybe you can arrange an acceptable party at your own home. The same goes for curfews, use of the family car, and other areas of negotiation. We need to be willing to listen carefully, communicate respect, discover the real issues, and compromise constructively. If we do this, rather than relying on one-sided decisions or engaging in a vicious round of arguing or character assassination, we will be well on the road to satisfying conflict resolutions.

Sometimes it is necessary to *agree to disagree.* Although the ideal would be to work out every conflict to everyone's satisfaction, we live in an imperfect world. There will be times when we cannot arrive at a mutual decision. When this happens, we may have to let our teenagers know that we are trying to understand their position, but we have decided we will have to do it a different way.

Let them know this kindly, and don't expect them to feel good about it. It is natural to get upset and feel angry, discouraged, tied down, or misunderstood—when you don't get your way on an important issue. Just try to be as kindly and sensitive as you can, and let them know that they have a right to their opinions. You just feel that this time, as their parents, you must make this decision. There are going to be other times when you have to let them make the decision, even though you do not agree. At those times you will need the grace to be willing to accept their autonomy, just as they must sometimes acknowledge your responsibility!

23

Teenage Negativism

Now we come to a problem that is more serious than the periodical disagreements and conflicts which every parent encounters. What about a teenager who is constantly negative and troublesome? He lets us know he thinks we can't do anything right. He sasses us. He rebels against our standards. And in a thousand little ways, he gets under our skins and makes life miserable. We try everything we know but nothing seems to work. Even if things get better for a while, he soon reverts to his old patterns. Sometimes things get so bad and teenagers become so negative their parents wish they would leave home to provide a little relief from the constant tension!

Problems like this are not healed easily. If you are caught in this type of struggle, you may as well face the fact that it won't improve overnight. Problems like this have generally been coming on for years, even though they apparently showed up suddenly. Sometimes they are the result of years of parental pressuring and coercing. Sometimes they are the result of "temperament clashes." And sometimes they are the result of serious problems in our family living and communication. But whatever the cause, this sort of ongoing fighting will not give way to a couple of new ideas, gimmicks, tricks, or lectures. It also will not be solved by adding new rules or restraints, or by dropping old

ones. It is indicative of strong feelings of anger and resentment, and these emotions aren't readily resolved. In fact, above all else, constant bickering and negativism in young people is a sign of anger at us for the way we are relating to our offspring. This does not mean it is all our fault. But it does mean these conflicts can never be resolved, unless we are willing to look at part of the problem. It is much like marriage. There is no such thing as a marriage problem where only one party is in the wrong!

Sometimes we get so exasperated that we blame everything on our teenagers. We may even tell them, "I don't know what to do with you!" This only makes matters worse. It is our way of saying, "Don't blame me for your bad attitude. I have done everything I can. Now it's up to you!" But this isn't really helpful. If we are going to resolve this type of conflict, we must be willing to be ruthlessly honest with ourselves and look closely at our part in the situation.

If you find yourself engulfed in this type of battle, it is time to stop, turn, and plan new strategy. When two people are at sword's point, no real victory is possible until at least one is willing to step back, analyze the situation, find out what the problem is, and then attack the real problem rather than its symptoms (or the other person!). Most attempts to handle teenage sassing, negativism, and rebellion fail because they are directed toward relieving outward symptoms, rather than the inner problem. We want to stop the sassing, or smoking, or sullen negativism. Perhaps we want to stop "that horrible music." But these are only symptoms. They are our teenager's way of saying, "I am angry! There are things going on in our relationship that I do not like." And underneath this message is a genuine desire to solve that deeper problem.

Now I realize that "genuine desire to solve the deeper problem" may be totally out of sight to you! In fact, all you can see may be a stubborn, disobedient teen, who seems bent on his own or your destruction. But if you step back long enough to observe your child's unspoken messages, you will find that deep down he is longing to be loved. He craves your acceptance and approval. The problem is that years of hassling over small things, or of contradictory or repressive directives have confused or enraged him. If he acts like he doesn't love you, he probably is convinced you don't love him. These feelings, compounded by all of the other pressures of adolescence, can make for very trying times!

This condition usually calls for the help of a more objective third party. Sometimes a professional counselor is needed. Sometimes an observant good friend can give a clue. In either case, *we need a listening ear.* We have probably had a hundred suggestions from well-meaning friends. Right now we don't need more advice; we need a chance to talk. We need a chance to let someone know how totally frustrated and defeated we really feel. This may take hours, or weeks or even months! But not until we come to a point of some relief and self-acceptance will we be able to turn and more openly consider new insights.

The second step in solving this chronic crisis is to better understand our own reactions. Why does this child bother us so much? Why is he so difficult for us to manage? Do we have an excessive need for obedient, dependent children? Can't we endure impoliteness? Do we detest an unusual habit? If so, why?

No one enjoys these irritants, but for some reason they may bother us more than the average parent. Perhaps our parents didn't allow any expression of anger or frustration; or we may have wanted to rebel a bit and always suppressed it. Whatever it is, we need to come to an understanding of our part in the problem and the reasons for our strong reactions.

The third step in breaking a cycle of negativism is to begin to understand the reasons for our teenager's upset and frustration. It often helps to go clear back to the beginning. Frequently children like this have always seemed just a bit different. They have always been somewhat unpredictable, or they have had a long-standing personality clash with one parent or the other. Perhaps the child was born with a little different temperament, or perhaps the child is a lot like the parent he is in conflict with. The parent sees a bit of himself or herself in the child and doesn't know how to handle it; or perhaps this child is like the other parent. The traits in the child that the mother cannot stand are those she dislikes in her husband! Sometimes teenagers really get on their same-sexed parent's case because they are in a sort of competition for the other parent's love. A teenage daughter, for example, may resent her mother's closeness to her father. She is now becoming a young woman and wants to feel appreciated. Since her major yardstick for comparison is her mother, she continually finds fault and puts her down. In so many words she is saying, "I could do a better job than you!" In much the same way, some boys have conflict with their fathers.

Whatever the cause, the origins of our teenager's negativism need to be traced as far back as possible. As we do this, we can periodically ask ourselves, "I wonder how John [the "problem" child] must feel?" We must work hard to put ourselves in his shoes. We must think, *If I were his age, with his parents and his siblings, living in this town, and attending this school, how would I feel toward my parents?* Sometimes this seems impossible, perhaps because we are actually feeling a great deal like the child inside, but are used to repressing our negative feelings. In other cases we may not have experienced such feelings at all, if we grew up in a home where everyone routinely cooperated, and things nearly always went smoothly. Another parent or an outside party can often help us see how our teen might feel. Frequently the other parent has felt exactly the same way as our child!

Just as the process of ventilating our own feelings may take weeks—or even months—the process of learning to understand our teenager's feelings will extend over some time. Bit by bit the pieces fit together, and we start to sympathize, instead of recoil in our emotions.

Sometime in this process we need to sit down and have a long talk with the so-called problem child. By then we will have realized that the problem is not "a problem child." The problem is one of poor communication or relationship. It is a problem of two people who seriously misunderstand each other and who are goading each other.

Once we begin to see things this way, we can approach our teenager and say, "You and I really have a conflict going! I have been doing a lot of thinking and I'm trying to figure out what's going on. I would like to have a little talk and ask you to try and tell me just how you feel."

If you get any kind of a positive response, you might go on to say, "Today I really don't want to try to solve anybody's problem—either yours or mine. I have just realized that sometimes I have a really hard time understanding you. Maybe we are too much alike, or maybe we are just too different, but for some reason I think I really haven't been hearing everything you've tried to tell me. I know you may not want to talk a lot, but I am wondering if you can tell me a little how you feel about the way things have been going around here lately?"

Once your teenager begins to tell you how he feels, you are really on your way. But be careful. Do not judge, evaluate, criticize, condemn, or in any way suggest that his reactions, thoughts, or feelings are either right or wrong. Right now your goal is understanding. There will be plenty of opportunity later to talk about what is desirable and undesirable, but until you hear each other out, you have little basis for conclusions. Hopefully, your first talk will lead to others.

After two or three good chats, your teenager may even be ready to listen to how you feel! At this point, it is crucial that you tell him exactly how you feel, but that you take complete responsibility for your feelings. Your feelings, you see, are yours and your teenager is not responsible for them. He does not "make you angry." Looking at it that way puts the blame on your teenager for your feelings. A more accurate way of looking at it is that you respond with anger to his actions. That places the responsibility where it belongs. *We* are the ones who respond with anger, guilt, or fear.

When your teenager has had a chance to express his feelings fully, and when you have begun to really understand his emotions and ways of looking at things, then you can begin to share your feelings. A helpful way of shifting to your own feelings is to say, "I really appreciate your letting me know how you feel. I think I am beginning to understand. I would also like to let you know a little about my feelings." As you proceed, make it clear that you are sharing, not judging. You are communicating with a new respect for each other and trying to find a solution to your problem.

Once we have been able to express our feelings and frustration, we are ready for this next step. That is to *tell each other how we respond to the other's feelings and wishes, and begin to formulate some remedies.* At some point in our sharing, we will begin to sense that we are ready to ask the other's forgiveness, or to reaffirm our love, or suggest some steps that can help avoid future hassles. At this point a little informal contract or agreement might be helpful. We might decide on a signal our teenager can use when he begins to feel us pressuring him. A teenager might agree to simply raise his index finger to warn the parent bad weather is brewing. The parent might stroke his nose when he detects a bad emotional smell rising. We can also agree to try to control and gradually alter harmful attitudes or manners of speech. The goal is teamwork in moving ahead.

This brief survey of handling teenage negativism and personality collisions cannot totally prepare you to solve a long-standing problem. It does, I believe, outline general features of a workable plan for ameliorating or resolving these destructive patterns. If you need further help, seek out a competent counselor to help both you and your teen back on the track of family harmony and growth. The time and money spent will be more than repaid in increasing family unity!

24

Post-High-School Years

Many sons and daughters finish high school and go away to college or hold a full-time job and move away from their home. Some teenagers, however, continue living with their parents as they attend local college or hold a local job. They choose to save money by staying at home; or they might just pass the time in leisure, while waiting for a new inspiration to overtake them! This raises a few new questions in the teen-parent relationships.

Our teenagers are now legally adults. They have been driving for two or three years. They are old enough to vote, to join military service, and buy alcoholic beverages. Legally, they can come and go whenever they wish. If you have a good relationship with your late-adolescent, and if he shares your Christian values, the years between high school and marriage can be a very satisfying period. You can take pleasure in his increasing maturity. You can watch with interest his vocational and premarital development. And you can have a new level of fun as one adult to another.

If things are going smoothly during this period, you will have an opportunity to help your offspring in their vocational and educational planning. You can serve as a sounding board for their ideas and can offer some helpful suggestions, based on your own perceptions and experiences. You may also have an opportunity to assist in their selection of mates.

They may feel free to tell you a little about their "serious interests." Often a young adult goes through some rough waters and faces some tough decisions at this stage. They may weigh the advisability of getting married right away versus waiting until they are more established in a job or further along in school. They may break up an intimate relationship after several years of dating, or they may consider joining the military, or moving across country to be with a friend. If we have maintained a good relationship, we can often help with a listening ear or a well-considered impression. We must remember, however, that they are no longer children. As adults, they should make up their own minds since they will have to live with the consequences.

Sometimes, however, problems in family living arise because your teenager is still living at home, although he is legally an adult. He may, for example, decide that he likes to smoke. He may decide that he wants to return home at all hours of the night. And he may want to invite in noisy friends. Questions of paying for room and board and college and of attending church may also become sensitive issues. Two overarching considerations should be kept in mind: though your teenager is your child, he or she is no longer a child; you are also an adult with certain rights and prerogatives. Forgetting either of these confuses the functioning of the relationship.

Let's begin with the handling of finances during this period. Unless your post-high school adolescents are working in your family business, it is generally best that you not provide them with all of their financial needs. By this time, they are old enough to hold a job and at least take care of their own spending money and car expenses. And if they are working in a family business, it is probably best to pay a regular wage.

If your teenager is going to college, it seems to me you should help him as much as possible. If he can handle his studies and a little social life, and also hold down a part-time or summer job, he is doing well. Some college students have to divert so much energy to secure monetary help that they miss out on some of the most useful experiences of college living. The extremes of over- and undersupply should be avoided.

Some parents dole out thousands of dollars for tuition, a car, plane tickets home at every vacation time, and all the spending money requested. This uncritical handout stunts a collegian's growth toward maturity. The opposite error is to send off our offspring entirely on their own. Some parents think this will teach their children responsibility. It may, but it is more likely to assure their dropping out of school or getting under inordinate pressure. If you are able to help your children with college, do it, but be reasonable. Let them take care of some of their money needs, and let them plan a budget with you that will reasonably cover their college expenses.

If your older adolescent stays at home, another question that comes up is paying for room and board. I would suggest the following approach. If you need the financial assistance and he can afford it, it is logical to agree on a modest sum. If he had to rent an apartment and pay for his own meals, he would have to do it out of his own pocket, so it seems fair to pay you a bit. On the other hand, if you really do not need the money and think that it will simply be a good exercise to teach your son or daughter to be more responsible, forget it. This is not the time to teach him to be responsible. Remember, he is now an adult. If you could get along fine without his money, let him spend it as he wishes. Hopefully, of course, he will save a little to prepare for marriage or further schooling. But nothing will be accomplished by forcing him to pay rent when we both know we don't need the money. As a matter of fact, this may create resentment. Your son or daughter will know you are just trying to teach him or her a lesson or hold a little leverage over him or her.

"I said, isn't it wonderful to have Junior home from college"

Smoking and loud music are other common complaints of parents with post-high-school young adults still living in the home. Since they are now adults, should we assume that they have the right to do exactly as they please, wherever they wish? Definitely not! If you were renting a bedroom out to a stranger, you would probably talk with him ahead of time. If you are a nonsmoker, you would make sure he was willing either not to smoke at all in your house, or at least confine it to his room. You would also agree that he could listen to music in his room, but that it would have to be quiet enough not to disturb other members of your family. If we would agree on a few such natural considerations with a total stranger, we certainly should not apologize for doing the same thing with ours sons and daughters.

Sometimes we are afraid to bring these matters up for fear of creating anger or resentment. But if we do it on a rational, adult level, it is an entirely normal thing to do.

Of course, we cannot tell our young adults what kind of music they can listen to and whether or not they can smoke. They are adults now and that is up to them. We are simply saying that since we have privileges too, we are going to exercise a couple of them—the right to not have our home smelling of cigarette smoke, or the right to not have to listen to loud music that gets on our nerves!

Curfews are a little different matter. Most paying boarders would have the right to come and go at any time, except as unusual hours became disturbing. However, it seems to me that it is reasonable to have some limits. Although they cannot be hard and fast, they should at least tell us when they intend to return home. And we may be able to agree on a general sort of limit. The reason for this, once again, is not because we are trying to parent them and keep them out of trouble. By this time they do have the right to come and go as they please. The reason for this time limit is to alleviate our own anxiety. As parents we are likely to worry if our sons or daughters keep coming in at all hours of the night. No matter how well adjusted we are, and no matter how adult they are, it is normal to be worried if you wake up at three o'clock in the morning and realize your son is not home yet. If he is living in his own apartment that is entirely his business. But since he is still living with us, the effect of his behavior on us must be taken into consideration.

Attending church together as a family is another issue that sometimes confronts families with young adults. Earlier, I suggested that with younger teens we should make every effort to find a church that meets their social as well as their spiritual needs. I also suggested it was reasonable to ask teenagers to attend church once a week, even if they aren't too keen on the idea, especially if they choose the service. By the time our offspring are through with high school, however, it will do no good to try and bargain with reluctant attenders. At this age, they need to face the responsibility of their spiritual choices. We can still have an influence by being sensitive, warm, and communicative.

We could discuss several other issues, but by now the principles should be plain. At this age we must acknowledge the right of our offspring to make their own decisions. If they choose to live in our homes, however, we should exercise the rights of mature adults that are beneficial to us all. We should sit down and talk these matters through as one adult to another. If we hit some big problems and find no way to resolve them, we may decide it is time for the fledgling adults to strike out on their own. We should not decide this in anger, but we can simply talk it over and see if we can come to a mutually satisfactory solution. If they say they are going to continue to come in loaded at all hours of the night, we may simply have to tell them we cannot allow it. They must make their own decision: either be willing to show us a little more concern or find a new place where their life-style won't be continually unsettling others. Outside of a few extreme situations like this, we should be able to resolve most other issues easily.

25

What to Do After You've
Blown It!

For twenty-four chapters we have been discussing parental relationships with teenagers. We have looked at some of their unique needs and interest, and we have seen some ways of building positive, enjoyable relationships with them. Yet no matter how much we love our children, and how well intentioned we have been, many parents will still face difficult times when our teenagers reach their young-adult years. Some of them will go through periods of mild rebellion. Some will withdraw into a shell and refuse to communicate. Some will become involved in drugs. Some will move out of our homes in anger. And some will totally turn against us or our moral and spiritual values. The conflicts will vary in severity, and the casualties may be relatively small in number, but some very sincere and concerned parents will inevitably face these cruel disappointments.

As I talk with parents from all walks of life, one of the most difficult questions I am asked is, "What do we do after we've blown it?" Hardly a month goes by that the parents of one or more older teenagers do not come to me and ask this question in one form or another. Sometimes they say, "Is it too late?" Or, "We see now where we have been wrong." But in each case they are wondering, "Is there anything that we can do *now*?" In other words, they want to get beyond their past mistakes and failures and try to do something positive to rebuild a shattered relationship or overcome the effects of perhaps years of less-than-ideal training.

I answer immediately that *there is hope!* As long as we are breathing, we can change for the better. And the same is true of our sons and daughters. At this stage, it may be hard, and improvement may be slow in coming. But if we are open to needs for growth by ourselves and our teenagers, there can be progress.

Taking Our Share of Responsibility

The starting point for coping with any problems with our young adults is to take a hard look at our own personalities and life-styles, and try to determine as accurately as possible how we have contributed to the problem. No matter how much responsibility our offspring must bear, there is no denying that after fifteen or twenty years of living together, we parents have been very instrumental in the formation of our teens' characters. When there are problems, the first place to look is not the school, the church, the peers, the devil, or the society. God has given parents the basic responsibility for rearing children, and we should begin the analysis of our offsprings' problems with self-examination.

I suggest taking time with a mate or a couple of friends who know us well to retrace our parenting experiences. We need to ponder the good times and the bad. We need to identify when problems first became apparent. And we need to recall what was going on before they came into full view, since those conditions may have been, in part, responsible.

Further, we need to delineate our own personalities and the nature of our conflicts with our children. Which parent got along better with which children, and why? Were we overprotective, overindulgent, or overly authoritarian? How about underattentive, underappreciative, and undersupportive? Did we take time to listen from the time they were very young? Or were we too busy with our tasks or "the Lord's work"? Did we value their opinions and give them an opportunity to participate in family decisions? How pleasant and secure was the emotional atmosphere in our home?

We need to be painfully honest in this examination, in order to discover the real problems. The purpose is not to find causes for blame and guilt, but try to see with our teenagers' eyes the conditions that drove us apart or compounded problems.

Forgiving Ourselves

Closely related to our search for causes of our young-adults' conflicts or problems is our need to learn to fully accept the fact that we are sinful human beings, who will make mistakes, but can be fully forgiven. If we have not already settled this matter, we should take time to enumerate and confess our specific failures with our teenagers to the Lord. We should ask forgiveness for our long-standing irritability, our overly busy schedules, our refusal to listen, our domineering attitude, or whatever seems to have alienated or erected barriers between ourselves and our offspring.

Once we have done this, we should thank God that Christ has paid the penalty for these sins and failures. Long before our children were born, He knew we would make mistakes and He has paid the penalty for our misdeeds. We need to accept this forgiveness, in order to relate positively to our teenagers. As long as we are relating to them on the basis of guilt, we will never make much progress. We will try to relate to them differently, because we feel like failures and want to overcome our guilt, instead of acting out of love and a concern for their welfare. And they will sense our negative motivation. A teenager can spot guilt motivation a mile away. When we are at peace with God and ourselves, we are free to start building new and improved relations.

On several occasions I have seen parents try to solve problems or misunderstandings with their young adults out of underlying guilt. Feeling distressed over the discord and pain, these parents approached their son or daughter with great anxiety. Near tears or distraught, they revealed strong feelings of remorse and failure. They apologized profusely and almost begged their teenagers for forgiveness. They were very sincere, but their attempt at conciliation didn't work.

The son or daughter immediately sensed the parents' concern was not primarily the young adult's welfare, but their own. The burden of failure as a parent was weighing so heavily, the parents were desperate to remove it. Changes were imperative for the parents' sake, not the children's, and the parents' plea was rejected.

When we have learned to accept ourselves with our weaknesses and failures, however, and have received assurance of God's forgiveness, we can approach our young adults with increased confidence and strength. We can honestly and genuinely seek to establish a better relationship. We aren't pleading or moaning, but we are maturely looking to the future. What's done is done. It will certainly influence the way we think and feel today, and it may have really harmed our offspring. But it does no good to keep moping about and condemning ourselves for the past. If we are going to be more helpful in the future, we must learn a new style of relating. Discussing our feelings and experiences with another couple is one of the very best ways of putting this entire process in perspective.

Learning to Listen

When we have begun to understand some of the areas of our family life that contributed to our teenagers' rebellion, and have accepted ourselves because God accepts us, it is time to approach our offspring and ask for their input. They will, of course, not be excited about this prospect. They are too used to being lectured, reproved, or advised, and they are expecting more of the same. But if we make it clear that we are not going to try to change them or straighten them out, they will probably give us a chance. We can frankly tell them we have been thinking back over the past and realize there have been a lot of problems. We can say we realize they will be going on their own before long and we want to try to learn from our experience. We realize we have made some mistakes and had some problems. We will not be asking them to change a thing. We are simply asking them to tell us how they feel. We want to try to understand them and our-selves better.

Even this introduction is likely to be met with skepticism. At this stage, they may not be interested in being understood or lis-tened to. For years they held out hope for understanding but now they have given up. What they want most, they feel, is to be left alone! But underneath their angry, sullen, or disinterested ex-terior, we have a very real ally. Every human being cries out for love and understanding, especially from his parents. Even though there are strong feelings of resentment and a background of conflicts and problems, our teenagers still have a desire to be understood. They aren't about to let us know it—but it is there! And if we parents are really changing, it will gradually reveal its presence.

During this first talk, it is probably good just to ask your teen-agers how they feel about family life. Tell them you would like to know what things they would like to see changed, and what things could make for a more enjoyable life together. Don't get all syrupy and say you want everything to be beautiful. That would be too great a shock, or simply incredible. And don't tell them it's not too late to have the ideal family! At this point we are just trying to make a beginning. We are trying to start to solve a few problems rather than change the entire family.

The opportunity here is twofold. The first is to allow our teenagers to express their complaints and their desires. The second is for us to really hear what they have to say.

During this first discussion, we need to prove we are ready to listen in a new way. If our teenagers suspect we are just using a new format to apply an old tactic, it is doomed to failure.

This leads us to a very important understanding. Most young adults who have conflicts with their families and other problems of adjustment do not need more information from parents. Their basic problem is usually a relational one. They are in a mess or estranged from parents because something prevented them from getting along with the people who should have meant the most to them. Since most of these serious problems are rooted in relationships, we must change our approach to the problem. When they were younger we could instruct, train, discipline, pressure, or coerce. Now we have to take a different tack. We must learn to *communicate*. We must learn to understand their feelings and perspectives. And we must gradually learn to work out cooperative, adult solutions.

Acceptance and Approval

One part of communication rebuilding comes when we understand the difference between acceptance and approval. A few years ago I counseled the mother of a seventeen-year-old girl who had moved out of the home and was living with her boyfriend. She was also taking drugs and rejecting her parents' spiritual commitments. For the better part of an hour this mother poured out her concerns. Finally she asked, "What can we do?"

Since we only had one session together, I had to be as specific as possible. I began by saying, "It seems to me, you must begin by learning to accept your daughter, just the way she is."

She looked shocked and said, "But I couldn't do that. I am a Christian."

It was my turn to be startled. Then I asked, "Mrs. S ————, how did God accept you?"

She became pensive and after some long moments replied, "Oh! I get your point."

This well-meaning mother had not learned to differentiate between acceptance and approval. She assumed that if she accepted her daughter fully and loved her just the way she was, approval of the daughter's life-style was implied. I suspect that it was the parents' inability to accept their girl exactly as she was in earlier years that motivated the grown daughter to turn to drugs and premarital sexual relationship. Unconditional acceptance from her boyfriend probably drew the daughter away from her home.

If we are going to restore broken communication lines, we must learn to love and accept our offspring *exactly as they are*, no matter how strongly we reject their life-style or commitment. Jesus didn't tell us we had to change our life-style to win His love. He loved us exactly as we were. In response to His unconditional love, we began to alter our behavior.

Becoming Peers

In previous chapters I have indicated that part of effective parenting is our ability to help teenagers move from the dependent relationship of a child toward independence of adulthood. Since young adults feel they have attained maturity, whether or not we think so, it will be to everyone's advantage if we can hurry up and overcome the last vestiges of childhood parenting.

Even if our young adults have married and rejected many of our values, we can still influence them positively if we learn to become good friends. Friends do not fuss over them, or preach and threaten. Friends accept as equals. This may mean finding new areas of common interest.

Grandchildren can be one of them! Occasional get-togethers—for holidays or casual events—give us opportunities to share good times. And even though we may not have any "serious" discussion, these times can help restore confidence and mutual respect. But be careful. If you fall into your old pattern, these will just become opportunities for more misunderstanding.

Sometimes it takes years to become friends with children we have hurt deeply. But if we are willing to make the effort, we will gradually see relationships restored. Only as this happens can we really begin to influence our sons and daughters again. And this time the influence can be different. It will not be a parent trying to change a child, but one adult offering another the best of his life. Here is what a girl in her early twenties wrote about some positive changes in her relationship with her father that came long after many parents have lost all hope.

> My dad is a very strong, authoritative figure, and I take after him somewhat. In order to break away and grow up, I had to fight very hard. But this rebellion was a new experience to my folks, and they often made me feel like I was a bad person. I wanted my Dad's love and approval very much, but it really seemed like he did not *like* me, and he disapproved of me. He *did* love me, but he rarely said so or showed it, so I had no indication that I was loved and okay.
>
> He told me recently he wishes he had been more physically affectionate to me during that time. He thinks it would have helped. It wasn't that he didn't feel like it, but he was afraid to touch his teenage daughter, who no longer had the body of a child. When he told me this years later, I almost cried, thinking of the many times I felt rejected by him. Although his bone-crunching hugs leave me breathless, it makes me feel so loved and special.

A Commitment to Change

One thread that runs throughout our discussion of influencing young adults is the need for increased sensitivity to our own weakness and a willingness to change. In Romans 8:28 Paul wrote what used to be for me one of the most frustrating verses in the entire Bible. He said, "And we know that all things work together for good to them that love God, to them who are the called according to his purpose" (KJV). I have seen Christians greatly misuse this verse. They naively say, "Praise the Lord," when anything goes wrong, in spite of the fact that inwardly they feel very differently. But if we understand this verse correctly, there is a great resource for coping with difficult situations. Verse 29 goes on to say: "For whom he did foreknow, he also did pre-destinate to be conformed to the image of his Son, that he might be the firstborn among many brethren." This is a key to verse 28.

Paul does not say all things are good. He is not naive. He does not suggest that a daughter's living with her boyfriend without marriage is a good thing. And he does not say the severe misun-derstandings and conflicts in your home are good. But he tells us we can have a positive outlook in these difficult situations, be-cause God can cause even difficult situations to work out for our good, as they help conform us to the image of Christ. In other words, Paul is saying: "I know you have difficult circumstances to face. I know you sometimes wonder how anything good could possibly come out of this mess, but I want you to know that God is working through all circumstances to help you grow and ma-ture. Even the most difficult situation you will ever encounter can turn out for your good, because it can help you become more Christlike."

In another passage (Ephesians 5:20), Paul says we are to "give thanks in everything." There is a paradox here, if we apply these verses to the problems of our young adults. Apparently our first constructive concern will be for ourselves and our attitudes. Paul

doesn't say we are to be thankful *for* our young adult's problems
and negative attitudes. He says we are to be thankful *in* them.
How? By being aware that this is an opportunity for God to teach
us to become more Christlike in wisdom and love. At this point
most of us probably feel, "That is fine, but right now I am not as
concerned with myself as I am for my son. I can always learn a
lot, but right now I really want to help my children." That
sounds really humble and is entirely normal. But for some reason Paul turns the emphasis around. He says, "No, your first
concern is *not* to see how you can change your children's situation. Your first responsibility is to see how you can grow and become more like Christ through this problem."

Most of us, you see, would rather focus on our teenagers'
problems than our own situation. We lament, "I have a problem
with my son or daughter," and anxiously search for a new tech-

I'm supposed to give thanks in everything?

nique or skill to change our offspring. This often obscures the deeper need: for parents to undergo some basic change in our attitudes and actions. The situation is much like overcoming diseased fruit on a tree. Picking off the bad fruit will not restore the good crop. Rather we must look at the root system of the tree, and try to get to the real causes. In my experience, nearly every instance of severe conflict between a teenager and his or her parents is either started by or strongly influenced by parental personality patterns. This generally means that this type of conflict will not be resolved through a little improved communication or discussion. If we are prone to excessive anxiety, rigidity, hostility, overprotection, or inability to understand our teenagers' attitudes and feelings, we parents have to undergo real personal growth to resolve these problems.

You may initially think that is very discouraging. "I have been this way for forty years, and it's not nearly as easy for me to change as it is for my son," you protest. Or you may think, "Perhaps we can hold on for a couple of years and then the problem will be out of the house." Would you really be satisfied to turn your back on this opportunity for growth? The Bible says God saved us and left us on earth, so we can develop and participate in His plan for this earth. And God often uses conflicts to bring out some of our growth needs. In fact, if it were not for the problems that arise in our intimate relationships with our spouses and our children, most of us would do little growing after we are married!

Waiting

Most of us can look back on our relationships with our own parents and see some positive changes that have come as the often-tumultuous times of adolescence have gradually receded into the background. Issues that seemed major then are somehow less important. Problems that then seemed critical have been put in a more realistic perspective. All parties concerned have been able to see some of our own immaturities in the situation and begin to forgive and forget.

Some of us remember how "smart" we were in college, and how little our parents knew at the same time! Somehow, however, our parents have grown brighter over the years, and we have accepted the fact that we really don't have all the answers ourselves! One by one, many of the problems of adolescence have either been resolved, outgrown, forgotten, forgiven, or accepted as an inevitable part of growing up.

When we are in the middle of rather serious parent-teen hassles, it is difficult to believe that they, too, will gradually be resolved—but many of them will. After we have done all we can to learn to relate in a constructive manner to our teenagers, and after we have sought out all the help we can, we can still gain added assurance. This assurance comes both from our awareness that God has not given up on either us *or* our adolescents—and from the awareness that growth does not end at eighteen or twenty-one or even twenty-five. Our offspring will continue to pass through important developmental steps as adults, and as they do, new opportunities for both personal and family growth will come.

When we survey our own hearts, we may find that we are still laboring under some of the same inadequacies that handicap our teenagers. Conflicts with our teenagers can be God's instrument to help us avoid going through the rest of our lives with emotional hang-ups. Realizing this, we can earnestly thank God in the problems we have encountered, because we will see the fruits of our own increased openness and fulfillment, as well as that of our offspring. And we can thank God, not only for our opportunity to influence our teenagers, but for their impact on our lives as well!

Index

Activities of teens, shared by parents 93, 94
  church 79, 94, 102, 130-134
  hobbies 79
  sports 77
Adolescent sex 105-111. *See also* Sexuality
Alcohol 121-127
  acceptance of usage by parents 123
  and biblical view of 125
  and emotional disturbance 126
  discuss without scare tactics 124
  seeking professional help 127
  usage by teens 9, 13, 63, 92, 121
Anger
  against parent and refusal to attend church 130
  of adolescent and drug usage 126, 127
  of adolescent and rebellion 115, 126, 127, 149
  of parent and punishment 115, 116
Anxiety of adolescents
  over dating problems 19, 41, 96, 99-101
  over physical looks 17-20, 40
  over sexual questions 19, 20, 41, 106, 107
  over vocation, college 20, 41
Appearance, physical, of adolescents 15-22, 40, 41
  emotional effect of 15-19, 29
Attitude of parents. *See also* Dating: Sexuality
  and commitment to change 168-171
  and discipline 117, 120
  and wedding boycott 104
  as "one of the gang" 78
  in accepting child "as is" 90, 166
  in placing the blame 148, 161, 162

should be positive 14, 41, 42, 117
toward church attendance 132, 133, 158, 159
toward teens' finances 136-140, 155, 156
toward teens' friends 90-92, 94, 95, 100
toward their own parents 75, 76
toward their own teen years 48-51, 82, 97, 110
toward today's adolescents 9-11, 31, 32, 41, 48, 52-54, 75-79, 80, 86, 141, 142
toward own sexuality 24, 61, 97, 106, 110
toward usage of alcohol and drugs 123, 126
when challenged 150
when child goes "too far" 110, 111
Acceptance by parents
  of teen "as is" 90, 166
  of teen's anxiety and discontent 47-54
Acne 19

Biblical absolute or parental interpretation 67

Cars
  "cruising" 103
  fast driving 63, 103
  ownership 66, 136, 138
  use of family 71-73, 103, 139, 145
Challenges of adolescence 10
Chores and concept of logical consequences 117-120
Christian parents
  and confession to God 82, 162, 163
  and teens' disinterest in church 128-135

differentiate between biblical absolute and own 67
reaction to sinful attitude of teens 57, 110, 111, 166
Christian teenager. *See also* Church
  and dating 101
  and peers 131
  and premarital sex 105, 108, 109
  church outings 102
  commitment to God 25, 109
  conflicts for 25, 31
  disinterest in church 128–135
  forcing teens to attend church 132–134
  search for spiritual identity 25, 41, 159
Christianity of parents, as viewed by teens 132–133
Church
  and the teenager 128–135
  changing churches 130–132
  dos and don'ts turn off 130
  forcing teens to attend 132–134, 158, 159
  reasons for disinterest 128–130
  rebellion against parents 36, 130
  selecting a service 133, 134
  youth programs 94, 129, 130, 132
College financing 139, 155, 156
Communication between parents and teens
  agree beforehand on discussion 142, 143, 152, 153
  avoid mixed messages 71–74
  discussing drugs and alcohol 124, 125
  give reason for decision 68, 73
  importance of listening 53, 54, 57, 67, 69, 81, 82, 110, 117, 142–145, 149, 151, 152, 159
  lack of 67, 76, 77, 93, 147, 164, 165
  openness in discussing sex 106–110
  prearranged signals for 153
  spending quality time important for 93
Companionship. *See* Parents as friends
Compensation by teens 18
Compromising 145
Confession to God by parent 82, 162, 163
Conflicts. *See also* Negativism
  as instrument of God 171, 172
  capitalize on areas of agreement 143, 144
  caused by extremes in setting limits 64–66, 69
  caused by identity search 42, 43
  compromising in 145

coping with 141–146
post-high-school years 160–172
rejection by parents 148
rejection of parents 36, 160
Conformity. *See* Peer pressure
Conger, John, on masturbation, *Contemporary Issues in Adolescent Development* 24
Contraceptives 107–109
Counseling 69, 70, 127, 149
Courtesies in dating 99–101
Criticism, effects of 61, 141, 142
Curfews
  after high school 158
  exceptions 119
  setting of 66, 71, 72, 103, 142, 143, 145
  violations and logical consequences concept 119, 120

Dancing, objections to 68, 130
Dating 16, 19, 25, 64, 96–104
  and curfews 66, 71, 72, 103, 142, 143, 145
  avoid preteen 101, 102
  girls dating older boys 16, 66, 103
  parent recollection of 19, 50, 110
  parents' concern about 96–98
  practical instructions from parents 99, 100, 110
  setting guides for 101–104
  single-dating age 104
  steady 98, 103
Decision making by adolescents 73, 74
  after high school 159
  in family matters 85, 86, 112
Development of parental role 75–79
Discipline 112–120
  and logical consequences concept 117–120
  avoid allowance withholding as 140
  avoid authoritarian methods 112, 113
  explanatory chart 116
  is not punishment 114–117
  of disciples by Jesus 117
  pattern set early 112
Disrespect for authority 9
Dreikurs, Dr. Rudolph, and logical consequences concept 117, 118
Drugs 9, 13, 63, 121–127
  and emotional disturbance 126, 127
  availability of 121, 122
  discussing without scare tactics 124, 125
  experimentation 123, 124
  parental attitude toward 123–126
  seeking professinal help 127

Eli and his sons 64
Emotions of adolescents 55–58. *See also*
  Mood changes
  effect of physical appearance
    on 15–19, 29
  empathy of parents important 12, 51,
    52, 57, 58
Empathy. *See* Understanding, parental
Enjoyment of children 10, 77, 93, 154.
  See also Parents as friends
Entertainment, forms of, approved by par-
  ents 68
Epithets 18, 83, 84, 141, 142
Excitement, teens' search for 63

Fantasies, sexual 25
Family relationships. *See also* Communication; Peer pressure; Relationships
  and openness about sex 106–111
  after children are married 167, 168,
    171
  importance of stability 25, 26, 92, 93
  set specific time to discuss prob-
    lems 142
  spending quality time together 93, 94
Father-daughter relationship 90, 167,
  168
Father-son relationship 23, 76, 77
Finances 136–140
  after high school 155, 156
  allowance method 137, 138, 140
  emergencies and special occasions 139
  for college 139
  jobs 137, 138
  parental handout 136
  parents matching savings 139
  "you're on your own" 136, 137
Firsts for teenagers 10, 21
Flexibility in setting limits 68, 101–104
Freedom
  should increase with age 68, 101–104
Friends. *See also* Peer pressure
  important part of growing up 98, 99
  parents as 75–79, 104, 166, 167
  parents should be hospitable 90–92
  teens' loyalty to 62, 92

God
  as loving, forgiving Father 111, 130,
    166
  uses conflicts for growth 168–172
Grandchildren as means of getting family
  together again 167
Grant, Wilson, on sex education, *From Parent to Child about Sex* 106
Guidelines
  for handling conflicts 141–144, 151–
    153, 164, 165

for maintaining good relations with
  teens 12, 112–120
for parents' commitment to change
  168–171
setting for dating 101–104, 110
teens still need direction 113
Guilt feeling of parents 14, 162, 163

Hair length 68
High school, the years after 154–159
  church attendance 158, 159
  decision making 159
  education 155, 156
  finances 155, 156
  legal adults 154, 158, 159
  living at home 154–159
Hope for parents of rebellious teens 161,
  166, 167

Identity, search for personal 30, 36,
  39–43
  cause for conflicts 42, 43, 75
  crisis for teens 39, 40
  crisis for parents 75
  dissatisfaction with self 39, 94
Independence, struggle for 34–38
  dependency of early years 34, 35, 75
  rejection of parents 36, 160
  regression 36–38
Indian Prayer 11
Intellectual peak 37
Intercourse. *See* Sexuality

Jesus Christ. *See also* Spiritual search
  and discipline of disciples 117
  and personal relationship with 101
Jobs for teens 137, 138, 154, 156

Limit setting by parents 63–70, 77, 113
  after a problem has risen 69
  after high school 154–159
  and future privileges 66
  avoiding extremes 64–66
  biblical standard 65, 66
  guidelines for 67–69, 101–104
  is sought by teens 64
Listening. *See* Communication
Living at home after high school
  advantages of 154, 155
  finances 155, 156
  possible difficulties 155–159
Logical consequences concept 117–120
Love. *See also* Family relationships; Relationships
  and discipline 114
  importance of expressing 43, 111, 149,
    164

Marriage, early 103, 104, 155
Masturbation 24
Maturation, physical
 of boys 16, 17, 22, 23, 40, 63
 of girls 16, 18, 19, 21–23, 40, 63, 101,
  102
Memory of parent's own teen years 15,
 19, 48–51, 74, 97, 110
Menstruation 23, 24, 29
Messages, conflicting parental 71–74
Mood changes in adolescence 27–30
 affected by new roles 29, 30, 36, 37
 are normal 29
 more prevalent among girls 29
 hormonal influence 29
Mother-daughter relationship 23, 150,
 151
Mother-son relationship 90
Movies, objections to 68, 130
Music, loud 9, 149, 157, 158

Narramore, Bruce
 chart showing differences between punishment and discipline, *A Guide to
  Child Rearing* 116
 on discipline, Help! I'm a Parent 112
Negativism 36, 134, 147–153. *See also*
  Conflicts
 breaking the cycle of 149–153, 171
 importance of communicating
  151–153
 reasons for 150, 151
 symptoms of 149
Nicknames. *See* Epithets

Parents as friends 75–79, 81, 82, 104,
 154, 155, 166, 167
Parties
 slumber 144–146
 unchaperoned 103
Paul, apostle, explanation of epistles
 Ephesians 5:20 169, 170
 Romans 8:28,29 168
Peer pressure 31–34, 89–95
 and Christian youth 25, 31, 94, 134,
  135
 is natural 32, 33, 89
 not necessarily harmful 89
 parent's own conformity to 32
 positive effects of 34
"Perfect parent" 14
Petting 110. *See also* Sexuality
Physical peak 37
"Pill," the. *See* Contraceptives
Pregnancy, unwanted 64, 107, 111
Prejudices of parents perceived by
 teens 62

Preteens
 and peer pressure 32
 parents of 14, 134
 should avoid dating 101, 102
"Problem" child 151
Problems of adolescents 13, 64. *See also*
  Conflicts; Negativism
 coping with 141–146
 do not appear suddenly 120, 134, 147,
  148
Puberty 15, 16
Punishment
 as result of parental anger 115
 as seen in Scriptures 114, 115
 explanatory chart 116
 is not discipline 114–117

Rebellion, adolescent. *See also* Conflicts;
  Negativism
 against church 43, 128–135
 against parental values 36, 147
 as result of punishment 115
 despite well-intentioned parents 160
 signs of 149
 use of drugs, alcohol, a form of 126,
  127
Regression 36–38
Relationships. *See also* Family relationships; Peer pressure
 and children's identities 33, 34, 42, 43
 and successful discipline 129
 maintaining positive attitudes under
  stress 104, 110, 111, 117
 of parents as friends to children 75–79, 104, 166, 167
 of parents to children of opposite
  sex 23, 90
Repairing earlier damage to parent-child
  relationship 160–172
 acceptance of child "as is" 166
 avoid self-condemnation 163
 confession to God 82, 162, 163
 parent commitment to change
  168–171
 parent share of responsibility 161, 162
Resentment of child toward same-sex parent 150
Respect, parents for teens. *See also* Relationships 80–86, 113, 141, 145
Responsibilities
 academic 29
 financial 136–140
 of children should increase with
  age 29, 68, 72, 117–120, 156
 parental 77–79, 146, 161, 162, 168–171

Ridicule. *See* Teasing
Room and board after high school 155, 156
Rule imposing after the fact 69
Rules. *See* Limit setting by parents

Sarcasm, effect of 61, 83, 84, 141, 142
Savings, matched by parents 139
Schedules of teenagers 47, 48
School activities important 137, 139, 156
Schools and sex education 108
Scripture
    1 Samuel 2:22–36 64
    Proverbs 13:20 89
    Proverbs 22:15 113
    Isaiah 13:11 114
    Romans 8:28, 29 168
    Romans 12:19 115
    1 Corinthians 9:20 145
    Galatians 6:2 82
    Ephesians 5:20 169
    Hebrews 3:13 94
    Hebrews 12:10 114
    James 5:16 82
    Revelation 3:19 114
Scriptural guidelines. *See* Biblical absolute
Second-guessing by parents 73, 74
Self-appraisal, by parents 83. *See also* Attitude of parents
Self-assurance
    and individuality 32, 43
    of both parents and teens necessary to avoid conflicts 42, 43
Self-condemnation by parent 163, 164
Self-control
    of parents under pressure 110, 111, 115, 116, 125, 148
Self-esteem 94. *See also* Identity, search for personal; Self-assurance
Self-hatred among teens 39
Sex education 105–110
Sexuality
    and fantasies 25
    and self-doubt 25
    and steady dating 104
    awakening of 19–26, 41, 106
    designed by God 106
    experimentation 63
    importance of openness in discussion 106–110
    information on sex from parents 105–110
    information on sex from school 108
    intercourse before ages sixteen and twenty 26
    masturbation 24

menstruation 23, 24, 29
    of parents 24, 97, 106, 110
    positive attitude toward 106
    premarital sexual encounters 26, 69, 103, 105, 107
    reactions to 21–23
Shoplifting 64
Signals, prearranged, for parent-teen communicating 153
Skills of parenting adolescents 11, 13, 14, 92–94, 166, 167
Smoking
    a sign of rebellion 149
    at home, after high school 155, 157, 158
Social relationships. *See also* Peer pressure
    importance of 102, 137
    linked to maturity 16
    search for 41
Sorensen, Robert, on early sexual intercourse, *Adolescent Sexuality in Contemporary America* 26, 105
Spanking not for adolescents 113
Spiritual search by adolescents 25, 41
    after high school 159
Standards, comparison and development of 68
Steady dating 98, 103, 104
Strommen, Merton
    on adolescent interest in opposite sex, as reported in *Five Cries of Youth* 96
    on self-hatred, as reported in *Five Cries of Youth* 39
Suicide 39

Teasing
    avoid 60, 61
    harm of 18, 19, 60, 61, 83, 84
Temperament clashes 147
Tithing for teens 137
Troublesome teen. *See* Negativism
Trust of parent 71, 72. *See also* Attitude of parent

Understanding, parental
    of differences in individuals 67
    of sensitive areas 59–62
    of teen conflicts and frustrations 12, 51, 52, 55–58, 69, 80, 128–131
Unpredictability. *See* Moodiness

Vacation planning a family affair 85
Values, parental 36, 94, 95, 147, 154
Vandalism 63

Wedding boycott 104